PILLOW TALK WITH THE KING

Estella Smith

Please direct all copyright inquiries to:
B.O.Y. Enterprises, Inc.
c/o Author Copyrights
P.O. Box 1012
Lowell, NC 28098

Paperback ISBN: 978-1-955605-22-9
Cover and Interior Design: B.O.Y. Enterprises, Inc.

Printed in the United States.

Dedication

I lovingly dedicate this book to Jesus Christ who put the desire in me to share his heart with other in hopes that it would bring inner healing to their soul. This project is only possible through the Holy Spirit gracing me to write as the pin of a ready writer upon the hearts of those who desire to have their encounters through intimacy by having Pillow Talks with the King! Lord I am truly grateful and honored. Thank you!

Table of Contents

Introduction

As a child, I always found an escape through writing. I had a vivid imagination, always looking to get away from some challenging times I had growing up. So, I was always writing down things that I would hear within me. But unfortunately, I had very little confidence and did not know how to articulate what I heard because what I heard came out of my heart. I didn't realize that the poems I called "thought" actually came from the Lord.

Words would fall off my lips from my heart to the pen, then to the paper that didn't sound like anything I knew to write. It was as if someone was whispering the words in my ear, and I would write what I heard.

One day in ninth or tenth grade, I wrote a poem and showed it to my 1st block teacher. I approached her reluctantly and asked her if she would like to read something, and she said yes. After she read the poem, she asked me who wrote it. When I told her I wrote it, she gave me this contentious look and said she didn't believe me. My heart and little confidence sank like the Titanic. I wrote less and less privately through my teen years, my twenties, and even into my fifties; it was like in the book of Malachi when God stopped talking to the children of Israel. He became silent for 400 years. I stopped writing for about thirty years.

The Lord sent me signs that I should write during this time, but I didn't receive them. The first sign was around 2000. My neighbor had a strong relationship with the Lord and was an intercessor, a seer, and a prophetess. I admired her and wanted to have the encounters she had with the Lord. One day, she gave me a prophecy and said I would write many books. When I heard her say that, the first thing that I thought of was the teacher in high school that made me feel humiliated and inadequate. I did not receive the prophecy, dismissed it, and continued with life as if I had not heard anything.

Every so often, God would remind me of the prophecy about writing. I would write things that I would hear in my heart, but I didn't keep the journals. As I moved, I would throw them away without understanding the significance of what the Lord was sharing with me. They were books, but I thought the writings were healing from something I was going through personally. I thought it was a private lesson in God just for me.

Fast forward to 2019. The Lord used a stranger during my visit to the Billy Graham Museum on July 4, 2019. I was walking around the museum alone and encountered two ladies from Raleigh. One of the ladies walked up to me and said, "The Lord told me to ask you why you have not written your book. Women are waiting on you. The book will be a legacy even when you are gone." I was stunned and caught completely off guard by what she said. I felt uneasy and thought this was a gentle rebuke from my loving Heavenly Father. He is still trying to get me to align with His purpose for my life.

I always cried to the Lord about wanting to fulfill my purpose but was not doing what he had asked me to do over thirty years ago. I did not view writing as my purpose and did not understand that I was disobedient regarding the instruction. God won't give you a new assignment until you complete what He told you to do the first time. Like the mother of Jesus said at the wedding in Cana, "Whatever He tells you to do, do it!"

In 2020, I repented to the Lord for being disobedient and not doing what he asked me to do many years ago. I never considered myself a writer; instead, I was recording what I heard in my heart. So, out of obedience to God, I have recorded these thoughts from the Holy Spirit, sharing them with you.

This book will inspire you and bring you into an intimate encounter with Holy Spirit. My prayer is that the words in this book will pierce your soul and facilitate your heart-to-heart dialogue with Holy Spirit. Holy Spirit wants to take you on a fellowship journey with Him and show you how to navigate life's challenges. "I will not promise you that life is smooth sailing," says Holy Spirit.

"Still, I can promise you that if you yield to my leading and prompting, I will teach you how to soar and fly, undergird you, strengthen you, and love you through life's challenges. I will encourage you along the way," He declares.

You may have aha moments during this journey. You may even feel emotions triggered by something said, but my prayer is that you will experience healing of the soul. I desire that you gain strength for this journey called life. I hope that through these writings, you can take the Holy Spirit off the pages of this book and make the Word of God final authority in every area of your life. You must know that the person of the Holy Spirit is a real person who wants to have intimate encounters with you.

Through my encounters of brokenness, hurt, character flaws, healing, and continual growth, you can look at life from a different perspective. I hope my experiences with God will help you reflect and see where you are in your journey with the Lord. If you are not a believer in Jesus Christ, I hope you will feel the love of God through these writings and desire to seek Him for yourself. I want you to know without a shadow of a doubt that He wants to wrap His loving arms around you and say, "Come on into my habitation, become my son or daughter. I have been waiting for you. Come into my presence and exhale from life's challenges. I am your bridge over troubled waters. Not only am I your bridge but your wellsprings of life, your living waters. Drink with me, abide in my presence and allow me to whisper in your ear. Open your heart and journey with me to a place of wholeness in every area of your life."

The following conversations are highlights of the mercy of the Father to His children. I call these encounters *Pillow Talk with the King*!

Crisis

I spoke to the Lord softly, saying, "Lord, I want to be more like you and desire to draw closer to you." I was meditating on things I was dealing with and vacillating about trust issues in my relationship with the Lord. I once had a stronger spiritual connection with the Lord and reminisced about that time. The darkness that had overshadowed the nations left me little time to doubt God or who He said He was in my life. Because a pandemic had spread globally, the coronavirus, lingering in the past, was not an option.

I heard about the pandemic in China in January 2020, but that was only in bits and pieces because I do not generally watch the news due to overly negative reporting. When I heard a co-worker talking more in-depth about the virus, I could sense the concern and fear in her demeanor and voice. She said she heard the virus had come to America. I began to think about prophets who prophesied in previous years that there would be plagues coming to the United States. I thought this was it! I searched Google to discover many people had died in China, and the virus was spreading. I immediately began to pray for my teammates, family, and the world. I decreed the blood of Jesus and divine healing and wholeness over everyone in the US and abroad. My first response was never fear, but instead to declare the Word of God and counter faith over fear. As I sat quietly at my desk, I felt like the Lord asked me, how will you stand? Without a shadow of a doubt, I knew that this was a test for me to see if I would walk in faith or fear?

Estella Smith

1 Peter 5:7 New International Version (NIV)

Cast all your anxiety on him because he cares for you.

The virus caused some people to fear and panic with uncertainty about when or if things will ever return to normal. The pleasures of going to the mall, visiting friends taking trips, and dining at your favorite restaurant ended abruptly until an unspecified time. It forced people to see what is essential and what is superficial. You can read the Word, attend church twice a week, memorize all the Christian culture and know what to say or do at the drop of a dime. Still, you know what spiritual deposits are seeded in you by the tests and your responses to them. How do you react in a storm? We can be taken aback by a sudden event and allow our emotions to overtake us. We must say hold up, wait a minute. I cannot allow this situation to engulf me in fear to the point that I cannot think rationally and not make sound decisions.

John 16:33 New International Version (NIV)

I have told you these things, so that in me you may have peace. In this world, you will have trouble. But take heart! I have overcome the world.

If the spirit of God is on the inside of you, there will be a quickening that will let you know, hold on my daughter, hold on my son; you were built for this. The Lord says, "Everything that you need to handle in a crisis is already in you. You were created for this. You must spend time with me and yield to my still small voice, and I will direct you through the storm."

There was a lockdown in the United States during the crisis, and certain restrictions were in place. One minute, people are laughing and enjoying life. The next minute, they panicked in disbelief that the nation had come under a severe attack by the enemy. It was an all-out call to prayer for the world. It was time to seek deeper intimacy with the Lord, forgetting about our inhibitions and what we think matters. Instead, we needed to focus on the things that matter most in life, such as family and friends, not material things with no eternal value.

The Lord allowed me to observe a myriad of emotions, from people's facial expressions to hearing conversations in a park one day. These emotions ranged from grief, fear, doubt, and unbelief, while some stood in faith, giving thanks to God and glorifying Him in the crisis. They trusted God for his divine protection, for food and shelter during this difficult time, knowing that He is greater than any circumstances or situation that would ever arise.

2 Timothy 1:17 New King James Version (NKJV)

For God has not given us a spirit of fear, but of power and of love and of a sound mind.

When the "and suddenly" arise, you will be tested on what you believe or said you believe. What you have allowed into your ears, eyes, and heart will come out of you. As the old saying goes, "what's in you" will surely come out of you. When trials test your faith, you will see what you are really made of. The Lord is a fruit inspector. He will come to try the Word that is within you. Are you ready?

The Lord says, "My son, forget not my law; but let thine heart keep my commandments. For length of days, and long life, and peace shall they add to thee." Proverbs 3:1-2 (KJV). God does not want his children to react to a storm in the same manner as an unbeliever. We must not live in fear and anxiety. However, you may have felt different emotions at the initial onset because of the unknown. That is perfectly understandable. But you must regroup quickly, reassess the situation, and know that your heavenly Father has it all under control. He is right there to be your rock, shield, and fortress. When trials and tribulations come our way, we must stand firm in our faith, giving glory to God.

When challenging situations arise, we often say it is the enemy, but that is not always the case. There are times when the Lord allows things to happen to us to activate our faith. We may not be relying on him in all areas of our lives. He may allow situations to occur to see what is inside of us. It could be bitterness, hatred, resentment, anger, etc. The Lord goes to the root and digs to uncover the seeds planted in us. Things we may not be aware of can affect the way we see Him, treat Him, relate to Him, grow in Him, and the way we may doubt

Him. He wants to pluck up and out of us everything that does not glorify Him. He wants us to examine ourselves in truth and allow the Holy Spirit to speak to our hearts. However, it is equally as important to yield to the instructions He gives to come into alignment with the creator.

Proverbs 3:11-12 New King James Version (NKJV)

My son, do not despise the chastening of the Lord, Nor detest His correction; For whom the Lord loves He corrects, Just as a father the son in whom he delights.

When turbulence happens unexpectedly and disrupts your plans, you may be disappointed because you have been planning and preparing for quite some time. As a result, you may become frustrated and feel derailed indefinitely or permanently.

Let us, for a moment, look at the pandemic crisis from a different perspective. Take a moment and look at any shift that has taken place in your life because of the pandemic. What was your response to the crisis? Was it anger because you may have lost loved ones? Was it fear of the unknown? If you lost your job, was it a feeling of hopelessness and helplessness? Perhaps you felt bitterness, anger, or doubt. Did you become lukewarm in your faith, or did you walk away from the Lord altogether?

I felt in my heart and heard the Lord say: "I came to shake the very foundations of the earth. I will expose, sift, and reprove the world. You must know that this crisis is not of me, says the Lord, but I will use it for my glory. People have put their trust in man and riches. They have made idols of themselves but lost sight of who I am. Do you not know that I am Jehovah Jireh, your provider? Do you not know that I am Jehovah Nissi, your banner, and my banner over you is love? Do you not know that I do my best work in crisis and calamity? I get to flex my muscles, and you will see my mighty hand move throughout the world and show myself strong on your behalf. This is but a small thing. What the devil meant for evil; I am turning around for your good.

Yes, this is a tragic situation, but I am in the midst of it. I create peace out of chaos and do all things good, not evil. I can heal your weary soul. I can heal your broken heart if you allow me to. You must trust in me even in this."

Put this book down at this very moment and begin to give God praise!!! It does not matter what the situation is; He walks with you every step of the way. If you lean into Him, He will give you the victory. Think about it. You were surprised, but the Lord knew what was going to happen. Take courage and comfort in knowing that when you rely on the Lord regardless of what is going on, the Lord will take care of you if you allow Him to do so. Romans 15:13 (Amplified Version, AMP) says, "May the God of hope fill you with all joy and peace in believing [through the experience of your faith] that by the power of the Holy Spirit you will abound in hope and overflow with confidence in His promises."

I hear the Lord say, "Rest in me." "My way is easy. When you lean on me and allow me to carry you, you can tread on the high places in strength, vitality, courage soaring like the eagle I created you to be. Rest in me, my child. I am your exceedingly great reward. My love for you, my children, is everlasting. Be not afraid of sudden changes, storms, and high altitudes of turbulence that are out of your control, for I am your landing pad for a smooth touch down and safe landing," says the Lord.

Prayer

Heavenly Father, in uncertainty, I will keep my focus on you. You are my guiding light. I bind the spirit of fear and lose the spirit of peace and victory because I am a world overcomer in you. Your yoke is easy, and your burdens are light. I will rest in you and find security in you in times of trouble, leaning not to my own understanding; in all my ways, I acknowledge you. I will allow you to direct my path and stand steadfast in you, the living Word, because I trust you, Lord. In Jesus' name. Amen.

Betrayal

Have you ever had a friend with whom you would share the intimate details of your life? Whether it was about your relationships, taking trips together, blessing them monetarily, sharing your most intimate personal secrets, etc., you confided in them. You considered them your best friend and a member of your family, an inseparable bond. However, as time goes on, you notice slight changes in the friend's behavior. You initially overlook it, but you know that the friendship is changing. Your best friend forever (BFF), who you called your "ride or die for life," is slowly distancing themselves from you. They do not call as much or want to hang out with you; there is always a reason, such as they are busy or something came up. They are evasive towards you. You feel you need to connect with them to clarify and understand what or if you have unknowingly done something to breach the friendship somehow. They appear unmoved by the fact that you are questioning the relationship. You begin to assess everything you did with them, the time you spent with them, and your investment in the friendship. You reminisce about the countless sleepless nights because you were counseling or consoling them. They did not think they could make it through another day, and you were there for them.

One day you hear that your friend spoke negatively about you regarding something you had dealt with in the past. You know it came from them because you only told them in confidence. You feel betrayed, confused, devastated, and emotionally abused. When you confront them, they don't deny what you heard. A myriad of emotions overtakes you. You are devasted! Holy Spirit tries to get your attention by speaking to you in the gentle voice you are accustomed to hearing. However, this time, you ignore His voice because you are upset. At that moment, you choose to bathe in the grief and pain. He continues to nudge you, but you become unresponsive to His voice and begin to shrink into your emotional state until your hearing becomes dull.

You know that the Word of God speaks on forgiveness. Matthew 6:14-15 (TPT) says, "And when you pray, make sure you forgive the faults of others so that your Father in heaven will also forgive you. But if you withhold forgiveness from others, your Father withholds forgiveness from you." Countless thoughts flood your mind about how and why this happened. Your immediate response is that you do not deserve this.

2 Corinthians 10:5 King James Version (KJV)

Casting down the vain imaginations, and every high thing that exalts itself against the knowledge of God, and bringing into captivity every thought to the obedience of Christ.

You have allowed the negative thoughts to take center stage. You are not in control of your thoughts, the enemy is, and he is having a field day with you. Does any of this sound familiar to you?

Betrayal takes many forms; adultery, sibling rivalry, problems with your job, problems in your marriage, betrayal in the church with relationships, leadership, etc. It does not matter what the scenario is; the pain is real.

In the 1990s, there was a popular catchphrase in the Christian circles, "What Would Jesus Do?" There was a lot of marketing around this phrase. There were tee shirts printed in various colors, car tags, and stickers on the cars displaying the slogan, and preachers incorporated it in many sermons. Let us take the phrase a step further. We know what Jesus would do for the most part in any given situation. Therefore, the subsequent response should be "Do What Jesus Did."

We discussed an example of a friendship betrayal. If you look into your personal life, you will see betrayal tailor-made for you by the enemy. This betrayal may have caused you to take your eyes off Jesus and focus on the problem. Without the Holy Spirit leading you in love, you can succumb to bitterness, rejection, unforgiveness, hatred, contempt, etc., towards a person or a situation you may be facing. Regardless of the scenario, what is your response to the problem? Ponder on that for a moment!

Yes, you were betrayed, and it will probably happen again. But, unfortunately, you are not living in a cookie-cutter world where everything is black or white. Many things will happen in our lives that may catch us off guard, and we may wonder why this is happening to us. We know that the enemy has come to sow tares in our lives and cause discomfort, pain, distractions, and turmoil. The enemy comes to disrupt the very nature of God in us if we are not mindful of his plots against us.

2 Corinthians 2:11, (NKJV)

Lest Satan should take advantage of us; for we are not ignorant of his devices.

Again, I will pose two questions to you, "What Would Jesus Do?" and did you "Do What Jesus Did!" First, are you attempting to protect your image or character by throwing up a defense mechanism or wall? Are you trying to avoid confrontation, disagreement, or confronting an issue because you do not want to be hurt again by someone you trust? Are you allowing a fortress of bitterness to keep you from receiving the deliverance that you need found in the Word of God? Do you get angry and seek revenge on the person who betrayed you? Do you get mad because someone has spit on your love? What is the pattern to all these questions? They all activate a response through your emotions. Will you choose the high road or the low road? You decide!

There is a lesson in every situation we face, should you accept this way of thinking. You can choose the high road of forgiveness, correction, Holy Spirit guidance, instruction, and love. Or you can choose the low road that leads to destruction, anger, unforgiveness, isolation and the list goes on. If you choose the high road, choose forgiveness, find solace in the Word of God and allow the Word to heal all the broken places in your heart and soul. Betrayal is a soul wound. Psalm 51:10-12 (AMP) says, "Create in me a clean heart, O God, And renew a right steadfast spirit within me. Do not cast me away from Your presence And do not take Your Holy Spirit from me. Restore to me the joy of Your salvation And sustain me with a willing spirit."

On the other side of the equation, after being hurt so painfully in whatever your scenario is or was, make the adjustment to regroup, gather yourself, and move forward. First, pause and take a moment to assess the situation because the pain is real. Then, you can talk about the problem with the person who hurt you and determine if the relationship is salvageable. Or you can release the person or situation from your life, tell them that you still love, and forgive them. Forgiveness releases you from the dilemma, not the pain; the pain will subdue over time.

In your intimate time with the Lord, allow the Holy Spirit to heal your heart. Ask Him to destroy the soul tie so that you will no longer be bound emotionally to the person or situation. Walk in love regardless of what your soul tells you and try to dictate your response or reaction. Do not allow bitterness and anger to consume you like cancer; that is what the enemy is banking on will happen.

God is your first defense in any situation. He knew this was going to happen; you did not. He is waiting with loving arms for you to invite him into the problem and open your heart to him. Matthew 6:33 (KJV) says, "But seek ye first the kingdom of God, and his righteousness; and all these things shall be added unto you." As you continue to seek the face of God in any situation, it will help you respond to negative situations appropriately.

Another way to help you heal from traumatic situations is to take your thoughts captive to the obedience of Christ. You do not want to entertain every idea that comes to your mind; they are not all your thoughts. The enemy has arrows shooting in your mind constantly, and it will be paramount that you differentiate whether they are your thoughts or the thoughts of the enemy. Let the Holy Spirit shine the glorious light of Jesus in your soul so that you do not stay wounded because of emotions you chose not to cast down. We must remember that all humans are fallible no matter how much we try to be as perfect as possible. Some people hold themselves to the highest esteem and highest standards with no room for error. However, man can and will fail you. Your anchor must be in the Lord who will never leave or forsake you.

Let me tell you about when I befriended Sharon (the name was changed to protect the individual's privacy). She was someone I mistakenly thought was my best friend. I gave Sharon clothes that I had never worn, drove everywhere we went, and paid whenever we went out to eat. I shared intimate moments with her only to find out she was an enemy to me. Through Holy Spirit and someone in leadership, I found out things were said about me that were not true. I remember hearing Holy Spirit tell me to pull away from her. Still, I rationalized she was regularly active in ministry; therefore, she wouldn't do something like that. I would ponder what Holy Spirit said but would dismiss it because I was looking at things from a logical perspective. What Holy Spirit said did not make sense to me.

I remember Holy Spirit distinctly spoke to me and said to memorize Psalm 91. He also instructed me to continually read Psalms 35 and 37 in the evenings when I came home from work. The voice of the Spirit would get louder and louder. The scriptures seemed to be warfare scriptures to me. But because I wasn't experiencing spiritual turbulence, I did not connect that He was trying to warn me of impending danger.

Another friend, who I will call Stacy to protect her privacy, would say there was something about my best friend, but she could not put her finger on it. She would always tell me my best friend was not trustworthy, nor was she a real friend. I ignored the warnings and would get irritated with Stacy for speaking against my friend Sharon. If truth be told, the comments were a hard pill to swallow. Holy Spirit continued to talk to me, but my discernment was off. I prayed all the time, so it was not strange for me to hear the voice of the Spirit, but I wasn't thinking clearly. I was confused, bewildered, and hurt.

When things came out into the open, I was devastated and hurt that someone I loved as a friend was my enemy. I went through literal warfare because of the manipulation I experienced. My soul was so distraught from the betrayal and bewitchment. I repented to the Lord for disobeying His initial instruction to sever the relationship. The Lord revealed I had developed a soul tie with her. I had to bind the soul tie and cancel its effects on my life. I sought Him throughout the year-long healing process.

I was only a few years young in the Lord and had not learned how to process the pain, nor did I have anyone to look to for guidance. I remember times when the Holy Spirit would check me because He heard the silent conversations in the depths of my heart towards her. I would never have known raw emotions like hatred were inside my heart. The Lord said I still needed to love her. I couldn't think or wish her evil in my heart. But, Child of God, the pain was real! I endured some intense months of tears, bitterness, and anger! I did not want to continue grieving Holy Spirit by dishonoring Him with my anger. I did not want to stay in the valley because the enemy was wearing me out emotionally. So, I asked the Lord to help me through this challenging season of my life. It was by the grace of God that I was healed! Christ Jesus gets all the glory, honor, and praise for His healing power and merciful love towards me despite my disobedience.

I can tell you that I know the Lord as a healer. The Lord would say, do not hate the person, pray for them, and I would communicate back to God; you do know what they did to me, right? The Lord would say to me; that forgiveness is not for them. It is for you. I would find scriptures on love in the Bible and recite and repeat them. Still, I could hear other conversations in my soul at the same time that were not edifying because of the pain. The Lord continued to walk me through the process. John Chapter 15 became my go-to scripture. I stayed close to the vine Jesus, and complete recovery and healing took place. I can tell you this. Please do not abort the process. If you need to cry, cry. If you need to vent to the Lord, there is nothing that you can say to Him that He has not already heard. He knows you better than you know yourself. He is waiting on you to release your burdens and cares on Him because He cares for you.

When trouble arises, always remember that according to Psalm 46:1 (KJV), "God is our refuge and strength, a very present help in the time of trouble." Seek Him while He is near; call upon Him while He may be found. Having a close relationship with the Lord can save you from battle scars and heartaches. Never allow anyone to block your love flow. Love is the most powerful currency of the Kingdom. After you have been set free, God will use your life to help set someone else free. You will have an opportunity to share the love of Jesus and speak about His grace to forgive others. You can share how you found the grace to forgive yourself for walking in disobedience, the power of repentance, and how he healed your wounded heart. You will have a testimony that love never fails, and the enemy is defeated. Stay connected to the vine, which is Jesus, and you will not just say "What Would Jesus Do?"; you will "Do What Jesus Did," love unconditionally. Choose love!!

Prayer

Father, I release and forgive everyone who has hurt me. I release them and do not hold on to present or past hurts that will keep me bonded to the enemy. I choose to be free because I am more than a conqueror in you, Christ Jesus. You have forgiven me of my sins, and likewise, I choose to forgive and walk in love with those who have hurt me. I release them out of my soul because I choose unconditional love! You said that if I do not forgive others, you will not forgive me. Therefore, I commit to being a vessel of love that you can flow through. So then, when storms arise and trials come, I know that I can do all things through Christ who strengthens me. In Jesus' name. Amen.

Fruit Inspector

When you go to the supermarket and venture over into the produce area and see the luscious red and green apples, grapes, pears, oranges, etc., whatever it is that whets your appetite, you may think about how the fruit is going to taste. You inspect the fruit to make sure that it looks healthy and appealing while still in the store. You look at the size, color, and weight, feel the texture of it; you may even smell it for freshness. You purchase the fruit with great anticipation of indulging yourself while satisfying your palate. You are looking at the outer appearance of the fruit by faith, hoping that it will taste as good as it looks. When you get home, you wash the fruit before eating it because of all the pesticides and other chemicals sprayed on it.

The same careful details and time it takes you to examine the fruit's outer appearance is the same way that the Lord wants you to examine your spiritual fruit. You must take inventory of the fruit of the Spirit according to Galatians 5: 22-23 (NET), "But the fruit of the Spirit is love, joy, peace, patience, kindness, goodness, faithfulness, gentleness, and self-control." You examine the fruit at the market with attention to detail and care because it will please you. God created all things for us to enjoy in the natural and in the spirit. Natural fruit is planted and must have fertilizer and water to grow. As you nurture the seed, it takes time to grow to its full maturation stage. When looking at things from a spiritual perspective, Jesus' character is the ultimate example of every fruit of the spirit. He embodies them all. Without the spirit of God inside of you, you will not be able to maintain the fruit of the Spirit.

Let's look at the first fruit of the spirit, love. You do not need to look any further than John 3:16 to see how God demonstrated the ultimate sacrifice of love through his son Jesus, the Messiah, the savior for the sins of the world. According to John 3:16 (KJV), "For God so loved the world that he gave his only begotten Son, that whoever believeth in him should not perish but have everlasting life." God, the creator of the universe, had a master plan to redeem the world back unto himself after the fall of man. God knew that it would need to be a person in His image and without sin. He needed someone who had His character to withstand the gates of hell, the trials and temptations, and the challenges faced on earth. Jesus watched His Father create the universe and worlds. He knew that His Father demonstrated and embodied love. Jesus knew that with His Father's support, He would fulfill His assignment because His Father bears much fruit.

1 Corinthians 13:4-5 (AMP) describes true love. It reads, "Love endures with patience and serenity, love is kind and thoughtful, and is not jealous or envious; love does not brag and is not proud or arrogant. It is not rude; it is not self-seeking, it is not provoked [nor overly sensitive and easily angered]; it does not take into account a wrong endured." I challenge you to think about how important love is; it is the bookend to all the fruit of the Spirit. It holds all the other fruit of the Spirit together. If you do not have love, the other fruit will not work. It takes love to manifest the other fruit of the spirit.

When we look at the scripture mentioned above, we will see and understand that Jesus holds Agape love to a high standard. We can look inwardly to see where we are in our love walk and ask the Holy Spirit to help us love like the Father and the Lord Jesus Christ. It may seem like walking in this type of pure, undefiled love is unattainable. If you look at this type of love in your strength and ability, you will not measure up to God's high standards. But when you say, Lord, I relinquish my will and allow you to take over the mountain or hurdle doesn't seem as high. You have the backing of the Holy Spirit to lead you in the way that is pleasing to the Father through King Jesus Christ.

Let us exhale right now and say, "Lord, have your way in my life. I decrease so that you may increase in me." Psalm 51:10 (KJV) says, "Create in me a clean heart, O God, and renew a right and steadfast spirit within me." Ezekiel 36:26 (KJV) says, "A new heart also will I give you, and a new spirit will I put within you: and I will take away the stony heart out of your flesh, and I will give you a heart of flesh." The only way that you can successfully walk in the fruit of the spirit is to live in the spirit. So please say these simple words, "Holy Spirit, let us take this journey together!"

The next fruit of the spirit is the fruit of joy. What is the first thing that comes to mind when you think about joy? Maybe laughter comes to mind, or perhaps you feel very peaceful in your soul.

What brings you joy? Take a moment and engage with that question. Receiving a gift, your children, a relationship, or your family may bring you joy. Now, let us look at joy a little deeper in the realm of joy activated by faith. If you are joyful based on how you feel, if something happens to disrupt that joy, you may become bitter, upset, or want to check out on God. That means your joy was only based on a circumstance or backed by your emotions which is temporal. Romans 15:13 (NLT) says, "I pray that God, the source of hope, will fill you completely with joy and peace because you trust in him. Then you will overflow with confident hope through the power of the Holy Spirit."

When you look at joy and inspect it based on the Word of God, the spirit of joy will always lead you to understand that the joy of the Lord is your strength regardless of the circumstance or situation. Whether you are in good times or bad times, the joy of the Lord is your certainty. The Word of God says, take my yoke upon you and learn of me. In hard times, look to Jesus, who is the author and the finisher of your faith. In the Word of God, you can stand confident in knowing that as Psalm 16:11 (NIV) says, "You make known to me the path of life; you will fill me with joy in your presence, with eternal pleasures at your right hand." Child of God, that means your joy comes from within, not from the outside, based on how we feel. God commands us to walk in joy, to live our lives in joy. God rejoices in His works and creations and expects us to walk in this fruit of the Spirit. Therefore, you must both abide in joy, cultivate joy, and guard your joy with all diligence.

Would you please indulge me as I venture off into a rabbit trail for just a moment? Nowadays, you must be incredibly careful who you listen to that teaches or preaches the Word of God. Some have enticing words that teach the Word of God but do not walk in the demonstration of the power of God. Some pastors teach the power of positive thinking, which can turn into a new age message about positive confessions and affirmations that may invoke another spirit if you are not careful. That spirit can manifest the answers to your prayers and confessions, but it's not of God. Listen to me, saints of God. If you are not speaking the Word of God in these affirmations, you could be opening channels for other spirits to enter your life. And yes, I am still talking about joy. Let me bring this into the context of joy. If you open the wrong spiritual portals, you may think you're experiencing joy because something you prayed for has manifested. But God is a jealous God, and He will not share His children with lesser gods or objects of their affection. Joy is the supernatural work of the Holy Spirit, and it is a spiritual attribute that manifests from the inside out. When you open spiritual portals from the kingdom of darkness, trust me, you will not experience permanent joy. Although you may feel a temporary pleasure, when Satan has gotten you hooked into his satanic web of deceit, lies, and bondage, you will have a hard time coming out of it. Then your joy will be disrupted by spiritual and natural anguish.

I've had conversations with people who ventured away from the Lord because their prayers were unanswered, or warfare became too much for them. They sought other ways or spiritual avenues to get their prayers answered. If you walk in offense with the Lord, you will not hear His voice because you are now walking in your sense and reasoning. If you are not listening to the spirit of God, let me ask you a question, what spirit are you listening to or obeying? If you have become lukewarm in your walk as a believer in Jesus Christ, repent for walking away from Him. The Word says He will never leave or forsake you, and He will forgive you. Psalm 51:12 (NET), says "Let me again experience the joy of your deliverance. Sustain me by giving me the desire to obey."

The next fruit of the spirit is peace. What does peace look like to you? Peace is that inner ability to trust the sovereignty of God under pressure and adverse circumstances. 2 Thessalonians 3:16 (TPT) says, "Now, may the Lord himself, the Lord of peace, pour into you his peace in every circumstance and in every possible way. The Lord's tangible presence be with you all." You can trust God no matter what you hear or see in the natural. You must continue to move on in faith no matter what. You are not easily moved or shaken by life's challenges.

Spiritual peace carries a hefty weight because you have grace under pressure. You must stand confident under pressure. There have been times when I experienced challenging situations, and I allowed my emotions to get the best of me because the test was challenging. The trial went on for a long time, or I did not put my complete trust in God in a situation. When I examined the fruit of peace, there was little. My armor was hanging to the side. I felt like I was on a spiritual respirator. I had to go into the reservoir of the Word of God or draw from my memory bank on a time when the Lord had graciously brought me out of a situation that I became frazzled in because I lost my peace. There are still times when I am wavering in faith about a problem. In those times, I must collect myself and realize that Jesus is the Prince of Peace. I repent and say, "I trust you, God." even if I am squirming in the process.

Let me tell you about a time when I allowed my situation to rob me of my peace. I worked a full-time job at a financial institution and had a little over an hour commute one way going and another hour coming from work to home. I worked the job for about two years, and the traffic was very heavy daily. The drive was very mentally taxing for me because the commuters were impatient, and so was I. I decided to apply for a job closer to my home to help elevate the distance and the time it took me to get home every day. I submitted many applications but only heard back regarding one position. It was a contract position at another financial institution. I contemplated taking the job. I prayed about the position, which would shave off an hour from my round-trip commute. Although I knew that it was not a wise decision, I accepted the assignment. It was supposed to be for twelve months with the possibility of another extension. I received a call from the agency during my third month informing me that they terminated my contract. The only thing that I could think of was I left my full-time position to take a substantial risk in a contract position. Although it paid more, I knew I made a grave mistake.

The day I received the call, I was not upset because I did not like the position. However, I knew I needed to hit the ground running immediately, looking for another job so that I would not use up all my savings to sustain myself.

Months went by, and I received no phone calls. I had no one to blame but myself for my decision, and I began to falter in faith and peace. There were times when I had a difficult time sleeping at night because I began to worry about paying my bills. I would be in faith one moment, then worry the next. I had worked so hard to get my credit to a certain point, and I could see that it was plummeting. I had a mortgage to consider. I had never been late on my payments, but now they were behind. I knew that I needed to change my approach because my emotions were all over the place. It took nine months to get another job, and my savings were tapped out. I remember saying, "Lord, I give this situation to you, and I am going to rest in you." The Lord came through for me! I shared my dilemma with a friend, and she told me about a program that could help me. I reached out to the agency and was approved. I did not have to pay my mortgage for a year! Praise God! I can tell you from that experience; that you can't buy peace. That is why I don't take it for granted. Peace is priceless. I had to learn to lean on God and rest in Him. He is faithful. Hallelujah!

John 14:27 (AMP)

Peace I leave with you; My [perfect] peace I give to you; not as the world gives do I give to you. Do not let your heart be troubled, nor let it be afraid. [Let My perfect peace calm you in every circumstance and give you courage and strength for every challenge.]

Peace is a spirit! When we rely on Jesus, he brings balance to us and restores our broken hearts and lives. When you think of peace, you may think of harmony, serenity, and tranquility. True peace is a state of mind where your emotions do not drive you. You are not looking at what's going on around you. Instead, you are governed by what's working within you, the Holy Spirit.

Romans 15:13, (NKJV)

Now may the God of hope fill you with all joy and peace in believing, so that you will abound in hope by the power of the Holy Spirit.

Longsuffering is another fruit of the spirit. When I think about the word longsuffering, what immediately comes to mind is how the Lord Christ Jesus has such grace of longsuffering for us whether we have asked Jesus to come into your heart or we are someone that is not presently serving the Lord Christ Jesus. He died for the sins of the world and knew that many people would reject him. We know that sinners sin because they do not have the spirit of Christ within them. Likewise, believers sin as well. The Bible says that we all fall short of God's glory. That is where the grace of God comes into play.

Psalm 86:15 (KJV)

But thou, O Lord, art a God full of compassion, and gracious, longsuffering, and plenteous in mercy and truth.

Longsuffering is what Jesus does daily. He watches from his place of abode in heaven at the people in the world who sin daily and still makes great intercession on our behalf, praying intently for us. I am speaking of a holy God that does not sin and hates sin but graces us by freely forgiving us of all wrongdoing if we would repent.

There may be times when you feel like the enemy is closing in on you from every side. You have prayed, fasted, and read the Word of God. You have your devotional times hoping you will hear a Word from the Lord that will get you out of the situation that you may be in at the moment. But it may seem as though the voice of the Lord is silent. You may feel as though you can't take the mental anguish, torment, sadness, or whatever you may be dealing with, and you are wondering Lord, where are you while I'm suffering. The Lord sees the end from the beginning. While our flesh is crucified in the suffering process, He is there helping us to endure the cross. He will never put more on us than we can bear.

1 Peter 5:10 (AMP)

After you have suffered a little while, the God of all grace [Who imparts all blessing and favor], Who has called you to His own eternal glory in Christ Jesus, will Himself complete, confirm, strengthen and establish you [making you what you ought to be].

The Greek word for longsuffering is long tempered. Think about that. Here are a few questions to ask yourself, and please be honest with yourself. Have you had dialogue with the Holy Spirit? He wants to commune with you. Allow the Holy Spirit to give you wisdom in the areas of your life that you need to mature. Do you wear your emotions on your sleeves? How do you manage your temper when something does not go your way? Do you give up easily when life happens, or sudden impactful changes appear that are out of your control? Pause to think of the outcome of your actions. Does it exemplify the grace that the Lord has given you to endure long-suffering? If not, you have time to make the appropriate changes and adjust your attitude, determining your altitude. If the Lord has forgiven us for all the times we have missed the mark; indeed, we can forgive others.

The following two fruits of the spirit are gentleness and goodness. I will speak about them together. Gentleness is the quality of being kind, mild-mannered, or tender. Times are profoundly changing, some things are for the better, yet some things are for the worse. I am sure that you can think of instances wherein the culture is morally declining in this day and time. Respect and honor for one another decreased significantly. As the body of Christ, we are to be the salt of the earth. We are to be the light in a dark, perverse generation. We must walk in the spirit of humility and meekness, be kind to one another, and love others as Christ gave himself freely for us.

Ephesians 4:2, (NIV)

Be completely humble and gentle; be patient, bearing with one another in love.

One of the beautiful displays of Jesus' gentleness was when He would hang around sinners, teaching them the ways of His heavenly Father. They were the ones society called misfits or castaways according to the religious sect in the Bible, the Pharisees, and Sadducees. Because we were a fallen people, gentleness does not come naturally to us. We must stay connected to the vine, the Lord Jesus, and read His Word so that we can walk in every fruit of the spirit.

I am not going to play religious games; there are times loving someone can be a challenge, and it takes the work of the Holy Spirit to help you navigate through your emotions. I have heard individuals say that they exemplified gentleness or humility but is that for the person to make that assessment about themselves or for someone to say that about them. We must be careful not to step into pride.

Gentleness is a surrendered heart to the Lord Christ and esteems others better than oneself. Jesus walked in every fruit of the spirit; however, when I think about the fruit of goodness, He deserves a standing ovation. He walked among those who hated Him, rejected Him, despised Him, and lied about Him. His enemies even spoke death threats to Him, but His loving kindness and tender mercies would cause Him to look to the heavens at His heavenly Father and say, "Father, forgive them for they know not what they do."

Romans 2:4 (AMPC)

Or are you [so blind as to] trifle with and presume upon and despise and underestimate the wealth of His kindness and forbearance and long-suffering patience? Are you unmindful or ignorant [of the fact] that God's kindness is intended to lead you to repent (to change your mind and inner man to accept God's will)?

Let that resound in your heart for a moment. If you are honest with yourself, there are times when you have directly disobeyed the Lord's instructions, and yet he continues to extend his goodness and mercy to you. Thus, the word of God says, the goodness of God leads you to repentance. God is the source of all things good. Goodness stems from Him, and we are a byproduct of His goodness.

In the book of John, a woman was found guilty of adultery. While those surrounding her were eager to punish her according to the law, Jesus did not condemn her for her sins. He kept His composure while looking down on the ground writing something, and asked those prepared to stone her, who of you is without sin, let him cast the first stone. One by one, the accusers dropped their stones and walked away, knowing that they could not deny their sins in the presence of holiness. Jesus looked at the woman and asked, "Where are your accusers?" He forgave her of her sins and asked her to go her way and sin no more. That is the goodness of God in a full demonstration. Jesus was always poised and confident under pressure.

Goodness and kindness go hand in hand. Kindness is the act of being kind and considerate, and goodness is the moral compass or virtues.

Pause right here and thank the Lord for His goodness and loving-kindness that He extends towards you every day, even when you did not deserve it. Then, inspect your fruit and see where you stand with the Lord. As I said earlier, be truthful about where you are and what you know needs to be changed in your life so you can be well-pleasing to the Father, Jesus, and the Holy Spirit. Can Jesus taste your fruit and find pleasure or disappointment, you decide?

Faith is the last fruit of the spirit in this fruit inspection. The Word of God says that it is impossible to please Him without faith. That is a powerful verse of scripture. Faith is the currency of the Kingdom of God. It took faith for you to believe in a God that you cannot see. However, we can all see the fruit of this invisible God through creation.

Ephesians 2:8-9 New English Translation (NET)

For it is by grace you are saved, through faith, and this is not from yourselves, it is the gift of God; it is not from works, so that no one can boast.

Romans 11: 1 (AMPC)

Now faith is the assurance (the confirmation, [a]the title deed) of the things [we] hope for, being the proof of things [we] do not see and the conviction of their reality [faith perceiving as real fact what is not revealed to the senses]. Now faith is the assurance (the confirmation, [a] the title deed) of the things [we] hope for, being the proof of things [we] do not see and the conviction of their reality [faith perceiving as real fact what is not revealed to the senses].

When you stand in faith, it means that you are relying on the Lord for everything. You have decided to submit your will to the Lord and wait on His timing to manifest what you desire. You live a surrendered life through faith because this is when you will see all the fruit in action. The more you trust the Lord, the more He will take you on faith journeys in Him. He will begin to groom you like He did Abraham, the father of faith. You may not always enjoy the process, but Galatians 6:9 (NLT) says, "So let's not get tired of doing what is good. At just the right time we will reap a harvest of blessings if we don't give up."

There are various types of faith listed in the Word of God. If you are a believer in Jesus Christ, the first type of faith is the saving faith. It took faith to believe in someone you could not see. Next, you may have felt the tangible presence of a loving Father through Jesus Christ by way of the Holy Spirit moving on you in love or conviction. The force of His love compelled you to come forward and accept Jesus as your Lord and Savior by the leading of the Holy Spirit.

Ephesians 2:8 (KJV)

For by grace are ye saved through faith; and that not of yourselves: it is the gift of God.

Then there is the fruit of faith that I discussed earlier in Galatians 5:23. An example of this level of faith is when you start reading the Word of God and doing faith exercises by concentrating on something and using the Word to back up your confessions. Then, wait on the manifestation of whatever you are believing.

The next level of faith is a measure of faith according to Romans. Jesus has given everyone a measure of faith to exercise and continue to grow that faith muscle.

Then there is mountain-moving faith. This level of faith reminds me of the centurion soldier in the Bible that requested his servant's healing. He had so much faith that he asked Jesus to speak the Word. He believed the Word of Jesus was enough to heal his servant. Jesus marveled at this Roman soldier's faith and said He had not seen such great faith in Israel. Jesus was saying the

Roman soldier had more faith than the children of Israel. His faith was great and unwavering.

Another example of this kind of faith was the woman with the issue of blood. In this era, if a woman were seen with that type of blood flow, she may be stoned or severely ostracized, but she felt within her that she would be whole if she could touch the hem of Jesus' garment. The tassels at the bottom of Jesus' garment represented healing. The woman had been to many doctors, and they could not cure her unusual blood flow. It is quite possible that she could have been one of the followers of Jesus or that she had heard of His notable miracles and the success rate of the testimonies. But, she knew this would be her opportunity for healing, and she didn't have anything to lose at that point. So, she went for it and pressed through the crowd of people. That took great faith because she didn't know if she could get near Him to receive her healing.

How many of us know that there is nothing the adversary can do to stop it when there is a divine destiny that God has appointed. The woman had a date with destiny, and the rest is history. Praise God! Saints, it is up to us which level of faith we walk in. Your drive, determination, and desperation for a closer, intimate walk with God determine your altitude in God. So, what are you waiting for? When we take on the characteristics of Christ, we must walk in all the fruit of the spirit. People will see the light in you even if they don't fully understand what it is. They may say, there is something about you, I don't know what it is, but you are different. Be the glory carrier representing Jesus!

Matthew 5:16 (KJV) says, "Let your light so shine before men, that they may see your good works, and glorify your Father which is in heaven." Jesus is the fruit inspector. What fruit will he find on your tree? Selah!

Prayer

Lord, I want to thank you for the many opportunities you have granted me. I must bless you and your Holy name. Blessing you has nothing to do with whether the circumstances are good or not. It has everything to do with you being the God that you are. I want to be a living epistle of the Word of God so that when you squeeze my fruit, all that you will hear coming out of me is the Word of God and faith. I want you to be able to say oh taste and see that your daughter is good, and the enemy has found nothing of himself in her. I bless your Holy name and will continue to yield to the direction of the Holy Spirit. I will learn from life's lessons, purified as pure gold for your glory. I will represent you with the fruit of the Spirit, and my fruit shall remain. In Jesus' name. Amen.

Right Thinking

The brain is one of the essential body muscles that must be stimulated and maintained to work correctly. In that brain is the mind, where you have your cognitive abilities to think, reason, and make decisions. Our actions are a direct result of our thoughts. It is your responsibility to monitor what goes into your mind. You are the keeper and steward of your soul (mind, will, and emotions). You must walk in dominion and take authority over your thoughts. John 10:10 (KJV) tells us, "The thief cometh not, but for to steal, and to kill, and to destroy: I am come that they might have life, and that they might have it more abundantly."

Abundance is not always about material things. If you do not have a prosperous mind, you are not living in abundance in that area. You cannot have a positive life but have a negative mindset.

You can listen to a person's conversation and tell what kind of attitude or mindset they have. Don't worry. There's no judgment here. I say this only to bring an awareness that the enemy is the master of throwing arrows, darts, and assaults at your mind. An example of this could be, you are doing chores around the house, and all of a sudden, a random thought comes to your mind that upsets or irritates you. Now you are taking offense about something that wasn't on your radar. Your offense is evidence of the ingenuity of the enemy attempting to seed a negative thought into your mind to see if you will take ownership of it. He hopes that you will accept that thought as your own.

Suppose you continue to ponder on that planted thought. That seed will grow if you water it with irritability, anger, etc. Then the enemy gets a foothold into your life. He will plant these thoughts into your mind, and if you're unable to discern what voice you're hearing, you take the thought and run with it. The danger of this is if you don't recognize the voice that is speaking the thought and never address it, it now can become a stronghold in your life. The Strong's Concordance says that a stronghold is a fortress, a strong defense. A fortress is a person or thing not susceptible to outside influence or disturbance.

Now, let us put this in context with the mind. Suppose you allow the enemy to continue to inject negative thoughts into your mind, and you do not cast them down. In that case, they become a fortress where you are deceived by the enemy because there is no light (the Word of God) sown into that part of your mind. Your mind then is defenseless against the enemies' attacks.

Romans 8:5 (NKJV)

For those who live according to the flesh set their minds on the things of the flesh, but those who live according to the Spirit, the things of the Spirit.

If you never deal with the mind, your life will never walk in the fruit that God intended for you. The constant bombarding of negative thoughts is spiritual warfare.

Philippians 4:13 (NIV)

I can do all this through him who gives me strength.

I will give you an example of constant attacks on the mind from the enemy in my life. I dealt with having a lack of confidence during various times in my life. I would attempt to do something and would hear you can't do this or that from the enemy. When I was younger, I always wanted to go back to school to get my Bachelor's degree but never did. So, when I reached forty, I felt that I was too old to go back to school. I thought that I would be unable to comprehend like the younger students just coming out of high school. When I would think about going back to school at that age, I would get knots in my stomach and feel anxiety because I wasn't sure I could do it. I was working a demanding job and could not see how I could put the time into studying. So, I would dismiss the thought, but my heart knew it was a goal I wanted to fulfill. I shared my secret with a few people who encouraged me to go for it. Unfortunately, I had committed self-sabotage and formed a mental stronghold over my comprehension and learning abilities. At that point, I had wasted five more years going back and forth in my mind about going to school in my forties.

One day I finally mustered up the nerves and confidence to call the admissions office at a particular school and set up an appointment to speak with an admissions counselor. I made a conscious decision to invest in myself and my life. I was going to do this!

I went back to school and received my Bachelor's degree in Business Administration, averaging a 3.5 GPA. I also received my Master's in Business Administration (MBA) with a 3.5 GPA at fifty years old! It was challenging working a full-time job and going to school full time, but by the grace of God, I did it, and it boosted my confidence. Please hear me when I say, with the thoughts and feelings that I described, you won't get anything accomplished.

If you do not learn how to master your thoughts and not allow your thoughts to master you, you are already defeated. You must anchor your mind with the Word of God. You must remember that you are fighting a spiritual battle. I also want to make a note that being around a good support system is imperative.

Ephesians 6:12, (NIV)

For our struggle is not against flesh and blood, but against the rulers, against the authorities, against the powers of this dark world and against the spiritual forces of evil in the heavenly realms.

Let me ask you a question. Have you allowed yourself to entertain thought processes that you knew were not your thoughts? What have you taken ownership of that has now become a stronghold in your life? What do you need to be transparent with Holy Spirit about so that you can confess, repent, and receive your deliverance? You want to have a prosperous mind, and the only way to achieve that is through the Word of God. There are times when we think that we can outwit Satan with intelligence or using our fleshly wisdom. However, he is a spirit; therefore, you must use spiritual weapons to defeat him. He must bow to the Word of God and submit to it. You subdue him by speaking the Word of God over the circumstances and situations you face each day.

Prayer

Heavenly Father, sometimes it is hard to see you in the midst of us seeing ourselves, living in our truths, and relying on our intellect to guide us. For this, I ask you to forgive me. Holy Spirit is the revealer of all truth, and my focus should be to make you Lord over every area of my life instead of trying to be lord of my life. Thank you for forgiving me when I miss the mark in you; likewise, you expect me to forgive others when they make mistakes as we all do. Lord, I will lean not unto my own understanding but in all ways acknowledge you and allow you to direct my path choosing the righteous path, which is to unconditionally love others as you so graciously love me. In Jesus' name. Amen.

Inner Healing

When you were a child, you may have played a game with your friends, and someone said something that upset you. They crushed your feelings, and you vowed you would never play with that friend again. But by the next day or sometimes within the same day, the two of you were back together playing as if nothing happened. Have you ever heard the phrase, "Sticks and stones may break my bones, but your words will never hurt me?" How many of us know that this is not an accurate statement? Words can be detrimental to a person because they pierce the soul.

Some people have gone as far as taking their own lives because of detrimental words spoken to them. You could be married or have been married, and your spouse broke your covenant. You put your whole heart into that person, and the betrayal felt like death. Maybe someone told you that you were not good enough, or you heard a family member say that you would never be anything, and you believed it. If you do not replace those negative words with positive affirmations, the voice that you hear the loudest is the one that you will obey. I want to say this, yes we can use positive affirmations, but they must include the Word of God. Only what you do for Christ will last. I am not speaking of a new age movement. I am speaking of the Word of God that breaks yokes and removes burdens. The anointing on the Word of God brings healing and deliverance to your soul, your innermost being.

Proverbs 16:24 (KJV)

Pleasant words are as a honeycomb, sweet to the soul, and health to the bones.

Another pain that one can experience is with silent words. You may ask, what do you mean by that? Have you been in a relationship with someone or talking with a close friend or family member, and there is a deafening silence? Perhaps you're trying to resolve an issue with them, but they are not responding to you. They know why you are attempting to communicate with them, and it feels like silent revenge when they are not responding to you. This childish act of silent treatment is manipulative and hurtful. At least when two parties are in dialogue with each other, you know what is in their heart, whether you like it or not.

When we hold onto hurt and pain for years and sweep the issues under the rug, we are not experiencing the healing that we need to live a healthy, productive life. When we have unresolved scars of our past or present, the wounds and trauma will continue into our future. Our heavenly Father desires that we are whole in every area of our lives. He dwells where nothing is missing, lacking, or broken.

3 John 2 (NKJV)

Beloved, I pray that you may prosper in all things and be in health, just as your soul prospers.

As you are reading this chapter, I want you to be open to experiencing inner healing in your soul. Psalm 34:18 (NLT) says, "The Lord is close to the brokenhearted; he rescues those whose spirits are crushed."

The Lord wants to minister healing to you. Allow yourself to go to an area of pain that you have suppressed. Ask the Holy Spirit to help you forgive the person that hurt you with negative words or whatever it is that has you wounded in your soul. Holy Spirit wants you free from the pain. Jesus took all the pain, burdens, and trauma to the cross so that you would not have to carry the pain. So please take a deep breath right now and invite Holy Spirit to go into the recesses of your soul. Invite Him into the places where you compartmentalized your pain and stored it in a closet in your soul. He wants to heal the crevices and cracks.

Begin the healing journey by admitting that the pain is there and begin to share your innermost pain with Holy Spirit. He is waiting on you. The process can be a long one because Holy Spirit must get to the root of the problem and begin to cut away all the layers that have been ignored for possibly a long time. Do not rush the process. Instead, embrace the healing journey that will result in the newness of life. The Lord came to give us life and that more abundantly to overflow. If the enemy can keep you in shame, guilt, and despair, he has a foothold in your life, and you are now at his mercy in this area of your life.

Isaiah 61:3 (KJV)

To appoint unto them that mourn in Zion, to give unto them beauty for ashes, the oil of joy for mourning, the garment of praise for the spirit of heaviness; that they might be called trees of righteousness, the planting of the Lord, that he might be glorified.

The Lord's arrows of victory are coming to you right now in the name of Jesus! Take your power back and make this confession: "Lord I am ready to be healed in my soul, and I cannot do it without you. I surrender." Next, take the time to reflect on what you desire to surrender to Holy Spirit and lay that at His feet. Allow Him to give you instructions for your healing journey and journal your experiences as you go so that you can see the progress that you are making every step of the way. In this way, you depend entirely on Him and are always in constant fellowship with Him. Whatever He tells you to do, do it. He will begin to work on inner healing that is tailor-made for you.

This journey may involve shedding many tears. It may open many wounds but remember that Holy Spirit is right there with you. The Lord is trying to delay everything that was lying dormant or suppressed due to the painful experiences you may have encountered. When you feel as if the intensity of the pain is too much for you, stop and exhale. At that moment, you may want to regroup and revisit your inner healing later or set aside a specific time another day to return to the place that you left off. It is essential to be transparent with yourself and stay honest with all your feelings, pain, etc. Get naked before the Lord in this healing journey, or He won't be able to heal you completely.

Everyone is not in a local body of believers where they have access to the pastor. Some individuals are not attending church at all. God gives us various avenues to get the proper help that we need, and one of those areas is counseling. I prefer Christian counsel, but each individual chooses who they select for their journey. You may be in such a deep place that it is too painful for you to tackle the inner hurt alone. The counselor will ask the right questions that will help you get to the root of the problem.

You must not check out emotionally. Get in the game and win. It is a fixed fight that you will win, but you must do the work. Take this moment in your devotional time and say, "I am worth the work that it takes to make me whole. Lord, I will forgive all who have hurt me. I will release the pain and trauma and will no longer allow it to take me captive. I will love unconditionally, even when it hurts so that I maintain the stewardship of my soul. Lord, I am ready to begin this healing journey with the help of Jehovah Rapha, the Lord, my healer, in Jesus' name."

I want to take the time to speak a few things over you as you go through your healing journey with Holy Spirit. First, you must accept the responsibility, ownership, and wherewithal to steward your soul. The Word of God says that you are fearfully and wonderfully made. Decree these affirmations: I am free from condemnation; I am victorious through Christ Jesus. I am purposely built and uniquely designed by God. I am a part of a royal priesthood and a chosen generation. All of my sins are forgiven. The blood of the Lamb redeems me. I am the apple of God's eye. The creator of the universe loves me, and He knows my name. He desires to be intimate with me and to bring healing to every broken place in my life. I am the righteousness of God in Christ Jesus. I am strong in the Lord and the power of His might. I am delivered from the powers of darkness and translated into the kingdom of God's dear son Jesus. I am God's workmanship created in Christ Jesus unto good works. I am the head, not the tail; above and never beneath. I decree restoration and healing to my heart, mind, will, and emotions. I will not accept the enemy's lies or allow anyone to disrespect me by calling me anything other than what and who God says that I am. I will cast down all negative thoughts and bring them to the feet of Jesus and not take ownership of them. I will continue to grow in the grace and knowledge of the Lord Jesus Christ. Hallelujah!!!

Continue to confess and read the Word of God and dig deep in your soul to allow Holy Spirit to uproot the pain and hurt in your heart. If you stick with the process, you will see the end of your faith manifested, and your testimony will glorify God.

Prayer

Heavenly Father, I exhale in you now. As I continue to abide in your Word and you abide in me, I can release my heart and allow you to create in me your clean heart and renew a steady fast right spirit within me. As your child, I will open myself up to you in transparency so that Holy Spirit can minister to me inner healing in the broken places of my life. I receive the benefits of salvation which includes healing and restoration of all things which is a part of the blood covenant as you died on the cross for me. I ask all these things in Jesus' name.

Romans 15:13, (NKJV)

May the God of hope fill you with all joy and peace as you trust in him, so that you may overflow with hope by the power of the Holy Spirit.

Forgiveness

Forgiveness is a soul-searching word. If you are in true forgiveness, it will cost you something. As I was writing this book, I encountered something that I have never experienced personally and was waiting for answers from Holy Spirit. When the Holy Spirit revealed this topic and I wrote this chapter, I examined my heart to see if I needed to ask for forgiveness or if I needed to forgive someone or accept someone's forgiveness. I want to be as authentic as possible and didn't want to write a book and not participate in the content myself. Know that I'm going through the process with you.

When I think about forgiveness, the first person that comes to my mind is the Lord Jesus Christ. He selflessly forgives us when we repent of our sins. However, He is not like us, who may hold a grudge when we become offended or hurt by someone's actions or deeds. Sometimes, a person can lash out at someone but not take the time to think before speaking. But to the person on the receiving end of that abrasive response, it may be painful. I am sure that we have all been there at one time or another. Whether you are the one lashing out at someone or on the receiving end of it, there should be an apology for hurting someone.

In the Right-Thinking chapter, we talked about "What Would Jesus Do?" Jesus would forgive someone who hurt Him and hope they would find it in their heart to forgive someone else without judging them. I know that this can be easier said than done. Sometimes, you can become angry at someone who is a repeat offender. Unfortunately, some individuals use the words "I am sorry" as a get out of jail card. They continue to hurt someone without really thinking twice about it because they know you will forgive them. Let's set the record straight. God did not call anyone to be a punching bag because they confess

Christ as Savior. You must have boundaries with this sensitive word, "forgiveness" yet, we must also walk in love.

Sometimes walking in love could look like you are distancing yourself from that person so that you are not always on the receiving end of verbal abuse or physical abuse. However, they may be lashing out because of soul wounds that need to be healed or considered. What Jesus wants us to do is get to the root of the problem in the soul by identifying the areas that need healing.

Luke 6:37 (NIV)

Do not judge, and you will not be judged. Do not condemn, and you will not be condemned. Forgive, and you will be forgiven.

Forgiveness is a matter of the heart. You may have dealt with a painful childhood, experienced divorce, infidelity, a friend's betrayal of trust, sibling rivalry, or a volatile relationship with a parent or loved one. Take a moment to look at the heart of the matter. The healthy thing to do is to release the pain and forgive. Sometimes the pain feels like you have been kicked in the gut and need a ventilator to breathe.

In a previous chapter, I spoke about inner healing. It is worth saying again; you must do the work. The more you practice forgiving someone, the less it hurts even if you did no wrong and it was the other person that caused the pain. Is it worth it to carry a grudge with someone and allow the pain and anger to eat at you on the inside like cancer? When you hold onto things inwardly, it can cause sickness and even premature death. Colossians 3:13 New International Version (NIV) says, "Bear with each other and forgive one another if any of you has a grievance against someone. Forgive as the Lord forgave you."

Let me tell you about when I struggled with forgiveness. I approached someone, who I will call Jessica (using a fictitious name to protect her privacy). Jessica and I were not friends. She was someone that I would speak to from time to time in passing but I knew she was very knowledgeable of the Word of God. I proceeded to ask Jessica a general question about something I was reading about that I did not understand. I thought she could shed some insight since she was the lead person over the prayer ministry as well as a minister of the gospel. A few days later, I received a call from the head of one of the ministries asking me if I was ok. My first response was, why did you ask that? To my utter dismay and disbelief, Jessica had a meeting with the pastor and said things to him about our conversation that was not true,

I was working in the ministry at the time, and my direct report leader talked to me about it. He stated that he had a meeting with the pastor, vouched for me, and told the pastor what was said wasn't true. I was so broken and hurt because the lie came from a leader who did not know me. I had a myriad of emotions going on all at one time. One was anger that turned into resentment and bitterness because of the pain from someone lying about me. I became withdrawn from the ministry because I did not believe that I could trust anyone in leadership. Weeks after the incident, I could feel bitterness rising in me whenever I saw the person.

Ephesians 4:31-32, (NIV)

Get rid of all bitterness, rage and anger, brawling and slander, along with every form of malice. Be kind and compassionate to one another, forgiving each other, just as in Christ God forgave you.

At home, the scenario played in my mind like a recording. I had a hole in my heart because I found out the minister was talking about me. I couldn't understand why the questions that I asked would lead to this outcome because to me the questions were not earth shattering. I just needed clarity about something that I did not understand which did not warrant this type of outcome. I would have negative thoughts about her, and I knew the Lord was not pleased with me. I was yet again wounded with a gaping hole in my heart due to "church folk."

I began to cry out to the Lord to deliver me from the hurt I was experiencing because I did not want to allow bitterness to take root. My emotions were controlling me and not me controlling my emotions. I remember telling a few people what happened because I was looking for guidance on how to handle the situation, but I knew Holy Spirit was not pleased with me asking others because he had already told me how to handle the situation, so I began to get quite before the Lord for continued guidance in the situation. The scenario continued to play in my mind on repeat like a broken record. I sought the Lord as my intervention to heal me of these deep wounds. How many of you know if you give the enemy an inch, he will take a mile if you let him. I could feel the enemy wanting me to retaliate and talk about the individual, but I never wanted to act out of character around someone, but more importantly, I didn't want to hurt or disrespect Holy Spirit. This was the opportunity to put in practice what the word says about the situation.

1 Peter 3:9 (NLT)

Don't repay evil for evil. Don't retaliate with insults when people insult you. Instead, pay them back with a blessing. That is what God has called you to do, and he will grant you his blessing.

I remember wanting to leave the ministry while in my soul-searching moments with the Lord. I began to aggressively pursue healing by first repeatedly asking Holy Spirit to help me forgive her. I am transparent here; this did not happen overnight. I had to go through several months of being processed through the pain because I would avoid her at all costs. I remember saying I would stop avoiding her and would speak to her because that was a part of my healing and forgiveness journey. When negative thoughts became persistent, I would cast them down. The more I made an effort to heal, the easier it became because I honestly wanted to please the Lord. I began to speak to her if I saw her. The key to forgiveness is you are not doing this for them. You are doing it for yourself. It took about six months for me to heal totally, but I did it by the grace of God.

I discovered that love and forgiveness are power twins. Isaiah 1:18 (NIV) says, "Come now, let us settle the matter," says the LORD. "Though your sins are like scarlet, they shall be as white as snow; though they are red as crimson, they shall be like wool."

Please remember no matter the offense, your ultimate goal is pleasing the Lord. In our flesh, we must die daily. You want to keep your crown clean and honor the Lord in your character. It is important to forgive. Mark 11:25 (NIV) says, "and when you stand praying, if you hold anything against anyone, forgive them, so that your Father in heaven may forgive you your sins." If you look in-depth at that scripture, you will know that your flesh is not worth the Lord rejecting you for all eternity. You don't want to be rejected by Jesus because you would not forgive someone for something they did, no matter how painful it is. It is not worth risking your salvation.

It is now reflection time. Think of someone you have not forgiven. Ask the who, what, when, where, and why questions as you allow Holy Spirit to minister to you. You do not need to do this alone; He is there to assist you in your forgiveness process. He is waiting on you to invite Him in. Get in a quiet place and clear all your thoughts and allow Holy Spirit to speak to you about whatever you present to him. One thing that you can do is instead of telling him what you want to heal from, ask Him what He wants to heal in you. Allow him to dig deep in the wells of your heart and soul. The key is to allow him to guide you and not you lead Him in the journey. Holy Spirit knows that you need healing and wholeness in every area of your life, but you can only truly focus on one thing at a time. You may be wanting the Lord to focus on one area of your life. Yet, He is drawing you to another area that may be weightier and may have more consequences. You are wondering why He is not answering your prayers regarding what you are petitioning Him for at that moment. If you need to, exhale through your tears, get a blanket and stretch out on the floor, whatever you need to do. Only you know how you meet the Spirit and commune with Him. Just release, let go and let God have His way with you.

Prayer

Heavenly Father, I want to take the time to say thank you for allowing me to come into your presence. In your presence is the fullness of joy. I take comfort in knowing that I can be transparent with you regarding anything that I am facing. Thank you for forgiving me of all my sins, Lord, and cleanse me from all unrighteousness. I know that there are times that I miss the mark and act out of character when I am hurt. I sometimes have hurt others with my word, deeds, and actions. I can come boldly to the throne of grace to find help and ask for forgiveness in a time of need. I want to exemplify your character, and I cannot do it without your help. Help me walk in victory each day and make a conscious decision to release the daily pressures. Then I can live a quiet and peaceable life of love and forgive others as you have forgiven me. You are the essence and embodiment of love, and because you are love, you forgive. I want to be just like you, Lord Jesus, and I know I can do everything with you. In Jesus' name. Amen.

God's Tapestry

What do you think of when you think of tapestry? It is a cloth that has been intricately woven together with certain specifications. It can range from different types of woven materials. The threads may be frayed and hidden in the completed work. In the process of incorporating different colors, patterns develop to create an exquisite, picturesque design. The detail and labor that goes into this type of artistry are time-consuming. But, when the product is complete, it is worth the pain-stacking effort and time it took to create the masterpiece. The quality of the material may range from cotton to silk material, with silk being one of the most expensive materials to use.

God created the human species as his masterpiece. He took the time to make us to his intricate specifications. We are made in the likeness and image of Almighty God. We are His prize creation.

Colossians 1:16 (AMPC)

For it was in Him that all things were created, in heaven and on earth, things seen and things unseen, whether thrones, dominions, rulers, or authorities; all things were created and exist through Him [by His service, intervention] and in and for Him.

When you think about the human specimen and the wonders of God's creative hands to sculpt a human being, it is breathtakingly awesome. Everything regarding the body has a function and a specific purpose.

Psalms 139:14 (NIV)

I praise you because I am fearfully and wonderfully made; your works are wonderful, I know that full well.

There are no words to describe the creator of the entire universe. He is a mastermind of all things. You may have heard the phrase, "jack of all trades, but master of none." You cannot master everything. If you had that capability, you would not need God. Instead, God has blessed you with specific giftings to cultivate with the help of the Holy Spirit. Use them how the Holy Spirit leads you as you walk out what the Lord called you to do before the foundation of the world.

When God breathed the breath of life into us, He saw Himself in us as a finished product of excellence and splendor. When He looks at us, He does not see a fallen man. He sees Himself through His son, Jesus Christ. Think about that for a minute. We are His handiwork, His tapestry. When someone weaves threads together to create the tapestry, they weave material close together horizontally and vertically in the same way God did with us. The artist hides frayed pieces of the thread in the tapestry so they are not seen on the surface. So likewise, the Lord covers our flaws and mistakes with His blood as we confess our sins and cleanses us from all unrighteousness.

Proverbs 28:13 (NIV)

Whoever conceals their sins does not prosper, but the one who confesses and renounces them finds mercy.

It can take months to complete a portion of the tapestry unless other artisans join together and help. Likewise, the Heavenly Father also has backup, Jesus, Holy Spirit, and angels to assist in a given assignment. Let us look at this from a natural perspective. Jesus hides us under the shadow of His wings and covers us while we are processed.

You should take the time to evaluate how special you are to the Lord. Know that all the things you have experienced, like the colors woven in the tapestry, are a part of your story, journey, and process to become God's masterpiece.

1 Corinthians 13:12 (AMP)

For now [in this time of imperfection] we see in a mirror dimly [a blurred reflection, a riddle, an enigma], but then [when the time of perfection comes, we will see reality] face to face. Now I know in part [just in fragments], but then I will know fully, just as I have been fully known [by God].

In your trials and tribulations, you are becoming the beautiful person He called you to be, but you must discern that He uses all things for His glory. You are that tapestry full of brilliant colors in the crayon box, a unique mix of different hues and shades.

I want you to ponder these things for a moment. Just as the threads are woven in the tapestry, you are intricately intertwined with the Father through Jesus Christ. You are fitly joined together in perfect alignment in harmony with Christ.

Ephesians 2:10 (NIV)

For we are God's handiwork, created in Christ Jesus to do good works, which God prepared in advance for us to do.

You are God's masterpiece. Stop complaining about what you do not like about yourself, how you wish you could be born into a different situation or circumstance, or look like someone else. When you say those things, you lose confidence in who God created you to be. Another thing, stop waiting on someone else to validate you when the Lord has called you to do something; that is an insult to the living God. You are created in his majesty and splendor just the way you are. Embrace your uniqueness and be authentically you. No one can be you. Someone can try to imitate things in your personality or style, but they can never be you. You are an original!

Estella Smith

If you are someone dealing with low self-esteem and always looking at someone else's life and saying, I wish that I were that person, pause right now. Please take a moment, go to the mirror, and look at yourself without makeup. Then say, "Lord, I am the apple of your eye, I am your royalty, I am the beloved of God, I am your favorite daughter." You are His diamond! He broke the mold when He made you. You are an original one-of-a-kind masterpiece, and He loves you.

There is a significant emphasis on weight, beauty, and size in the entertainment industry, which causes some teens to view themselves in a substandard way. That contradicts the Word of God and how He views His creation. The entertainment industry attempts to shape the views of those who will succumb to this subliminal undermining of subjective images that depict women and young adults in a certain way. I hear people saying, "this is their truth." I want God's truth more than I want man's truth. If the truth be told, all the subjective programming damages the minds of those who cannot discern the truth of who they are from the lie the enemy wants them to believe.

The Lord says, "I have put you on display for the world to see. Get off the shelf. Stop self-medicating. You are an original design. Walk in your splendor. Walk in the glory that I have placed upon you. If I am on the inside of you, how can you possibly think that you are a second-class citizen when I am the great, I AM, and you are my chosen vessel? Daughter, I want you to cultivate the things I have placed on the inside of you. Please read my Word and digest what it says about you. You must get the Word down in your spirit and meditate on the love letter that I have written about you and for you. I want you to know without a shadow of a doubt who you are in me. I want you to feast in my presence and learn of me. I want you to know your value and your worth according to my Word."

Joshua 1:8 (AMP)

This Book of the Law shall not depart out of your mouth, but you shall meditate on it day and night, that you may observe and do according to all that is written in it. For then you shall make your way prosperous, and then you shall deal wisely and have good success.

"You are greater than rubies, and I call you a queen. Hold your head up high as royalty that you were born into once you accepted Jesus as your Savior. Let me interject with this disclaimer, if you have not accepted me as your Savior, I love you unconditionally as well. Do not listen to the lie of the enemy or allow someone that is self-righteous to say to you that I don't love you because you have not come to me yet. I died for all mankind, no exceptions. I hope you would come to me because surely, I can take better care of you than the enemy. After all, I created you. I know what I have called you to and who you are from the inside out.

I showcase you as my tapestry for all the world to see. You are in my image and likeness. I call you forth now. Come out of the darkness into my marvelous light. I employ you to see who you are in me without hesitation, doubt, and fear. Be bold, be confident, be fearless. Radiate in the earth like the salt I called you to be. Don't make your boast in yourself; make your boast in me," says the Lord. "Sit back and watch what I will do in you, to you, for you, and through you," says the Lord. "You are my tapestry. Your footprint is in the earth for greatness; therefore, write author write, sing psalmist sing, play minstrel play, dance dancer dance, build constructor build, dream dreamer dream, and speak poet speak. Let the picturesque tapestry of your life give glory unto me in all the earth. You are my creation who was born to rule, to rein and give glory and honor to me the risen King. The Word of my power upholds you. Selah!"

Prayer

Lord, I give you praise, glory, and honor due to you and your holy name. Indeed, there is nothing made without you. I am your handiwork created in Christ Jesus unto good works. I am your masterpiece on the earth. Holy Spirit, help me to be the example and representation of Christ in the world. I am uniquely, fearfully, and wonderfully made in God's likeness and image. I am a daughter of Zion and will see myself the way that God sees me. Holy Spirit, show me how to allow my life to reflect the Word of God representing the finished product, the tapestry of the King of all Kings and the Lord of all Lords. In Jesus' name. Amen.

The Cross

The most incredible love story ever written is when Jesus went to Calvary's cross as a propitiation of the world's sins. 2 Corinthians 5:21 (NLT) says, "For God made Christ, who never sinned, to be the offering for our sin, so that we could be made right with God through Christ." Jesus carried the pain, sin, and offense of the world entirely in surrender and submission to His heavenly Father. He was fully obedient to every instruction that He heard the Father say, even death on the cross. Just think about it. What a selfless sacrifice He paid for the sins of the world.

In the Old Testament, the prophets would make an atonement to God by sacrificing animals on an altar, representing the sins of the Israelites, and offerings of thanksgiving for their victories in battle. Although the priest would atone for the Israelites' sins through repentance and the animals' blood, all of that paled in comparison to Jesus' sacrifice on the cross. Moreover, God would give the priest and prophets instructions on presenting the sacrifices to be well-pleasing to Him. They would be a sweet-smelling aroma ascending to heaven. They partook in all these rituals to receive the forgiveness of their sins. Still, how many of us know the partition, the wall, and the veil separating us from the Father tore on the cross. Now we have full access to Him through the atoning blood of Jesus, the Christ. Hallelujah!

Let us digress for a moment. Jesus lives in the third heaven, a place where there is unspeakable love, laughter, order, peace, joy, harmony, wholeness, holiness, and no sin. It's immaculate with a glorious splendor and majestic, awe-dropping beauty. He accepted the assignment from His Father to come to the earth and was rejected by man. Because He was slain before the foundations of the world, He did not come to the earth to complete his assignment blindsided. The most devastating part for Jesus was to be temporarily separated from His heavenly Father since they are one and have always been inseparable. Jesus was selfless, forgiving, loving, full of wisdom, and all-powerful. He was the God of all truth and brought correction and comfort to all who encountered Him.

Jesus was on assignment to transform the minds of the chosen disciples from an earthly mindset to a kingdom mindset to be effective disciples of the resurrected Jesus Christ. They would perform signs, wonders, miracles, and demonstrate authority and power, thus filling the great commission to become fishers of man. Jesus walked in kingly authority in the earth realm in submission to His Father through daily instructions, continual prayer, and communion with His Father without using His divinity. He was the epitome of righteousness and holiness, an excellent mentor and example for the disciples to follow. They gleaned from Him while taking on His characteristics by demonstrating exemplary leadership, humility, sanctification, holiness, righteousness, and wisdom. He is truly worthy of being praised.

This is not just a book; it is a worship experience. So, put this book down and give God praise for Jesus! Hallelujah!

We must never lose sight of the sacrifice that Jesus made so we can partake of His goodness and benefits during our daily endeavors. The world calls it a grind. As believers, we call it walking in obedience to the voice of the Lord. I wanted you to take time away from this worship experience to spend time in worship to the King of Glory because if it were not for Jesus, where would we be? It is not enough to say that you love him. You must demonstrate that love with your actions.

As I wrote this book, I paused to reflect on the goodness and grace of the Lord. I felt impressed to think about times when I opened the door to allow my self-indulgences to get the best of me, forgetting about the sacrifice of Jesus. Let me pause here and give a few examples of these self-indulges. When I was in my twenties through forties, I planned how I wanted my life to go and what I felt should be accomplished by a certain timeframe. I wanted the nice home with the white picket fence, the great career. I wanted to travel the world and enjoy life. There is nothing wrong with those things, the Word of God says He gives us all things richly to enjoy. But, I had not considered the plans that Jesus already ordained for my life nor was I asking Him those pertinent questions. All the things that I said that I had wanted, "the American Dream", of which some are still unrealized, became a barrier for me. I had too much emphasis on things of this world. I am not materialistic. That is not what I am trying to convey here, but what I am saying is that the sacrifice of Jesus on the cross far exceeds the things we want Him to materialize for us. He wants us to want Him in an abiding relationship with Him. There is nothing we're facing or have gone through that could compare to Jesus hanging on a tree in humiliation, being spat upon, and experiencing pain and agony for us.

We need to stay here for a moment and reflect on the mercy, goodness, and ultimate sacrifice of love He demonstrated for us. Hallelujah! Lord, we thank you for your selfless love toward us.

You can pick this book up or put it down at any moment in time. But I hear the Lord saying, "Stop what you are doing and worship me and my goodness. Look deep within yourself. I died so that you could live. I went to the cross in victory for you to destroy the works of darkness. I came to be the light of the world. Through this triumphant victory on the cross, you win!

This moment is about me. Stop, pause, and celebrate me. I repeat this is not just a book. I have risen with all power and authority in my hands. The cross was a heavyweight, and I could not have subdued it without my Father or the power of the Holy Spirit. How can two walk together except they agree? I agree with my Father, and I want you to agree with me. I am the vine. You are the branches and cannot abide outside of me.

I want you, my children, to reflect on a cross that you may be currently in or have been in and are now set free from. If you are currently in something overwhelming, where are you standing in this situation? Is it in victory or defeat? The times that you are the weakest, do you feel my strength? Do you hear my still small voice giving you instructions on how to take your next breath so that you are not overwhelmed? Do you understand that if you are carrying your cross, you are in disobedience to my Word? Have I not instructed you to give that to me? Lay your cares at my feet, my yoke is easy, and my burdens are light, is that not what my Word says? If you are carrying these burdens, my child you are not abiding in my Word or me."

Let us be honest here; this is your time of self-reflection as you progress through this chapter of the book. I do not want you to pick the book back up until you feel the release to do so because the Holy Spirit wants to minister to broken places in your heart. Allow Holy Spirit to wrap His arms around you. He is saying, "I love you, my child, even those that are not mine. I am here to minister to you through the pages of this chapter. When you have given me the time due to me, then and only then do I want you to pick up this book again and continue."

I hope you took advantage of the opportunity to commune with Holy Spirit and felt the power of everlasting love. If you are ready, let's move forward.

There were the naysayers in the New Testament, those who despised Jesus' teachings, wisdom, parables, and revelations. Some of the people who sent Him to the cross were Sadducees and Pharisees. They were well studied in the Torah, devoted to their studies, and prided themselves on their knowledge of God but had no relationship with the Creator.

The Torah was not inside of them. Although they sought and received knowledge, the words that they memorized never became a part of them or their lifestyle. They were not keeping even the ten commandments. They had no love in their hearts; therefore, when Jesus came to the earth, they could not discern Him or that He was sent by His Father. They felt it was their religious duty to send Him to the cross because they thought that He was committing blasphemy, saying He was the Son of God from heaven. They thought they were carrying a burden to get rid of Jesus because He was an offense to them.

Children of God, the enemy, will always have those on assignment to abort our mission. Those with hardened hearts are positioned in strategic places to oppose you while you are on your journey in God. The enemy will set up obstacles and arrows of darkness to derail you from your assignment. But let me interject this clarifying statement. Everything difficult in your life is not from the enemy.

We all have crosses to bear. Everyone's cross is different. It is tailor-made to your specific assignment. You were not born on the earth out of sheer happenstance. No, you were born for a divine purpose with an assignment to complete during your lifetime.

Whatever you have gone through or may be going through, the keyword is going through, not park and reside in the testing or trial; know that God is with you even when you cannot trace him. Sometimes, when you bear your cross, it seems as if Holy Spirit is a silent partner in the relationship. Still, it is in those times that He is watching to see how you follow His lead. He wants you to remember what he has spoken to you previously in your fellowship with Him. Listen, He does not waste words. He is the teacher, testing you and watching to see if you listened during your devotional or communing time with Him and through life's circumstances.

Jesus is the master teacher that gives many pop quizzes. Matthew 25:13 King James Version (KJV) says, "Watch therefore, for ye know neither the day nor the hour wherein the Son of man cometh." Matthew 24:44 King James Version (KJV) tells us, "Therefore be ye also ready: for in such an hour as ye think not the Son of man cometh." Typically, when you hear this verse, it is regarding the "Gathering or Rapture"; however, one scripture can have more than one revelation. It could mean many things. If you look at that scripture from a different perspective when He says, be also ready because you do not know the day or hour He comes. It could look something like this as well. Jesus is coming for His Word that He spoke to you. Think of it this way. He is coming for the fruit of the impartation. There is so much revelation in the Word of God that the Holy Spirit wants us to know yielded to His voice in intimacy. We cannot put Jesus in a box and think that we know the Word of God in its totality.

You must keep an open mind because you do not know how He will speak to you. You may be in the middle of doing something, going about your day, and sense a divine interruption of His still small voice. He begins to speak to you a phrase, a word, a vision, through the television, your pastor, a license plate, etc. He chooses the method at which He will speak to you, and it is up to you to be available, yield, and discern His voice. Yes, there are some individuals whom He speaks audibly as well. The method of communication is not as important as the fact that you hear Him when He speaks and obey that instruction. It is wisdom for your life and a divine encounter with Him. As He speaks, it is like building blocks as you obey. One instruction at a time is like building a plank in the spirit, and you walk on that plank in faith. Sometimes you cannot see the plank, but you will experience its effects as you obey. He continues to cause you to walk further in the realm of the spirit out into the deep. You will progress to levels and domains in the spirit based on your intimacy and obedience to His instructions.

Let us get back to the walking out of our cross. It is tough to see a loved one or someone you know going through something challenging, especially if it is your children or a close family member. You want to do whatever it takes to bring healing, comfort, encouragement, and deliverance to them from the situation. But maybe, just maybe, the person is in the position because that is their cross to bear. God wants them to know how essential He is to them, but they are too busy making their plans in life. God has no place in their lives. God desires intimacy with us. He is a jealous God and should not share His glory with another god or an idol.

God is either bringing you into humility or keeping you in humility. He is either bringing you into the fear of the Lord or keeping you in fear of the Lord. There are times when you are praying for God to change the situation to feel relief. Sometimes, He will bring instant healing and deliverance, but at other times He will not.

Isaiah 55:8-9 (KJV)

For my thoughts are not your thought, neither are your ways my ways, declared the Lord. For as the heavens are higher than the earth, so are my ways higher than your ways and my thoughts than your thoughts.

In those difficult times, we must trust the wisdom of the Lord. Who are we in our finite minds to think that we can instruct the Lord? He is the teacher, and we are the students.

Let us be honest for a moment. We have all been there where we are trying to tell the Lord what to do. How did that work for us? It behooves us to yield, child of God. It will surely lessen the blows of life.

When you are bearing your cross, do not fight God, it will only delay the process. You will end up staying in the testing longer than you should because you were or are fighting against your cross. If you are receiving the refiner's fire, let Him burn the dross off you so that He can purify you and make you white as snow. Do not despise the correction, the rebuke, and the chastening of the Lord. The Word of God says that He chastens those whom He loves.

Allow God to examine you in those areas of your life. Yield to the leading of the Holy Spirit for guidance and correction so that you can receive the resurrection power to overcome and subdue anything that the enemy is throwing your way. God will give you the grace to endure while you are experiencing your cross. Remember He is carrying you.

According to 2 Corinthians 9:8, (KJV), "God is able to make all grace abound towards you; that ye always having all sufficiency in all things, may abound to every good work." For example, suppose you destroy someone's process in your attempt to help or alleviate their discomfort or pain without understanding the Lord's cross for them. By prematurely helping them out of a difficult situation, you could destroy the righteousness that God was trying to fulfill in their life.

I am not saying you should not help those in need, but I am saying that you should be prayerful and seek God in all things. The person may have a cup to bear, and you do not want to hinder God's process that He is trying to take them through for their spiritual growth. Although things may be difficult for those you love, allow God's perfect will to be done in their life. When you discern that it is a cross, pray that the Lord will give them the strength, endurance, and the finisher's anointing to stand and the grace to endure their cross. If you abort their or your process, there will be another test because you did not receive the oil (anointing) for the test you were supposed to pass.

Psalm 138:8, (NKJV)

Estella Smith

The Lord will perfect that which concerns me; Your mercy, O Lord, endures forever; Do not forsake the works of Your hands.

The weight of what you are going through could be so intense that you have not discerned that it is a spiritual test. Therefore, you are fighting from a fleshly perspective and losing the battle. Child of God, anytime you are experiencing intense resistance in the natural, immediately seek Holy Spirit in prayer. It could indicate that it is a spiritual battle; therefore, you need to shift gears and seek the Lord for instructions on conquering this giant. Yes, you will carry many crosses in life. Still, the Word of God says in 1 Corinthians 10:13, (NLT), "no temptation has overtaken you except what is common to mankind. And God is faithful; he will not let you be tempted beyond what you can bear. But when you are tempted, he will also provide a way out so that you can endure it." Let us shout for the victory! The Word of God is true. Endure the cross, my child. Jesus assures your victory.

God knows what is inside each of us. He is not looking at us from a natural standpoint. He is looking at us from a spiritual perspective. So be careful not to slander God in your mind. You can do this when you are upset with Him or offended because He did not heal, deliver, or your prayers are unanswered or delayed. What we deem to be most important is not always crucial to Him at that time. For example, you are saying, "but God, this hurt so bad," or feel as though you will not make it. But God sees you have unforgiveness or something else in your heart that will keep you from advancing in your walk with Him. You are crying out in your flesh state, thinking you cannot take it, not another day, and He is saying to you, my grace is sufficient for you. You are saying to God, "You do not love me. Do you see my down here hurting?" But He is speaking to your heart, "Do you see that I cannot advance you in this state because you are producing fruit that is not of me. I want that to be removed from you so that you can spring forth as a well-watered garden in me.

God sees each of us from a spiritual aspect, not from the natural carnal perspective. He sees us in the book written about us in heaven before the foundations of the world. Praise God! When Jesus came to the earth, He would get alone with God, pray, and receive instruction for each day. His Heavenly Father would give Him instructions written for Him from the book of life in heaven every day. That is how He was able to win every victory, dismantle every enemy's plan, and carry His cross on the earth. Therefore, brothers and sisters, you must commit to spending quality time with the Lord each day, even time before the day if that is His instruction for you. Then you will not be a victim but victorious in every battle you face. You will be suited up for each day with the amour of God and ready to forge forth. Not looking at the cross you're enduring, but acknowledging the helper, Holy Spirit undergirding you to live a life of victory in whatever difficulties you may be facing.

God looks at our hearts. He knows our future, present, and purpose. My prayer is that your takeaway is that no matter what you are going through, do not pray that the Lord takes the cup away from you, but ask Him to give you the strength, grace, and fortitude to endure the cross. Ask for wisdom and understanding to pass the test you may be facing. Always remember when you come through the test to give God all the praise, glory, and honor. There is a reward on the other side of the test once you pass it. There are spoils, my child. Reap the rewards of your cross! Regardless of how uncomfortable you may be in your cross, pause for a minute and think of Jesus' suffering. Your perspective will change about what you are going through. God will always give you the grace to run your race. Trust in the Lord with all your heart and lean not to your own understanding. In all your ways, when you acknowledge Him, He will direct your path. Jesus loves you!!!

Prayer

Lord Jesus, I trust you even when I cannot trace you. Your Word says you will never leave me nor forsake me but will be with me even until the end. I receive the grace and strength from your spirit to follow where the Holy Spirit leads me because I abide under the shadow of your wings. I will embrace the cross with grace and strength in victory. In Jesus' name. Amen.

What is Love?

What is love? From a human point of view, you may look at love as erotica or something that entices your emotions. Some may equate love with being something that makes you feel a certain type of way. When you think of love from those perspectives, it can be an imbalance of emotions masked in conditions. Some may view love as if you do this for me; I will do that for you. It is all phileo, the type of love invoked based on one's emotions. Children of God that is not Jesus' type of love. His love caused Him to surrender His life to His heavenly Father, to fulfill a mandate on earth. He left the throne room and His Father to come to this sinful world.

The following is what the Lord is saying to us about love:

I knew that I would come to the earth to be rejected by men in my obedience to my Father. I would be spat on, hated, scorned, lied on, beaten to the point of being unrecognizable, and die all in the name of religion. When I came to the earth, I went with the grace of unconditional love that I learned from my Father, not the phileo love that humans knew.

My Father shows mercy, and mercy is love. My Father extends grace, and grace is true love, something you do not deserve. I love you because you are made in my likeness and image, not because of circumstances or situations. My son died on the cross for you, and it is only through my son Jesus that you have an opportunity to come and sup with me.

I release grace by the Holy Spirit to all humanity, those that belong to me and those that have no part with me. That is unconditional love. My desire for my children is that you will come and fellowship with me, although most reject me. Even those who say that they belong to me reject me. They have no concept of true love; they love what I give to them, though they do not deserve those things. True love is extending with an outstretched arm whether it is reciprocated or not. I continue to love the people, even those who do not belong to me, even when they reject me and my love because I am the creator of the entire universe. I love you all! If I bless you though you do not love me back or accept me, that is love. Love is also obedience. I am looking for obedience in my children, obedience to honor my Word and me, reverence me, and obey my commandments. Yes, my way appears structured, but there is a reason for it. I do nothing without purpose! I do nothing without purpose! I do nothing without purpose!

If I am asking you to do something, I have already foreseen something in your future that may be detrimental to you and the path that I have laid out for you. I know, see, and hear everything, even the plans, plots, tricks, strategies, and snares the enemy has set for my children. I am all-seeing and all-knowing, and nothing gets past my wisdom. My desire for you, my child, is that you would avoid the unnecessary pitfalls of the enemy. I will give you instructions that you can easily miss if you are not in tune with my frequency. The way that I speak to you may be through someone, something, through nature, the Word of God, worship, or praise. Do not think that you can determine or box me into a particular pattern or way that I will speak to you.

You miss my instructions, my children because you do not believe it is necessary to spend time with me. It leaves you an open target for the enemy. If you choose to take the time to commune with me each day, there is grace made available to you for that day. Each day is sufficient of its graces. Is that not what my Word says? When you preplan your day, you have omitted the anointing that I have made available for you. I give you the instructions, and you decide whether you will do them as you choose or not do them at all. When the enemy has sown tares into your day because you are uncovered, then you cry out for my help. The grace and mercy that you receive for one day will not be extended to you another day should you tarry. These are examples of my love.

As you can see, what you consider love to be and what I believe and know love to be are two different things. I do not love you conditionally. If I loved you conditionally, you would not be in existence because of the sin and rebellion that I knew about before the foundations of the world. I knew that you would do things that are shameful to me, but it is mercy and my love for you that covers you. Therefore, I will forgive you if you repent.

I created you knowing all things because of my love. It will benefit you more if you understand what true love is when you begin to harken to my voice, listen to me, seek me, pursue me, and call out to me. I am listening, and I am waiting for you. Yet, you are too busy for me, and you do not see me. I am not essential to you. You are not looking for me. My Word says you should not make this world your home. This is not your residence if you belong to me. You are a sojourner here on the earth, only passing through living on purpose. My child do not be a lover of this world system. Don't be deceived by what it dictates and its standards. I have so much more in store for you. You can live from a heavenly perspective. That is what my love came to provide for you. Seek the things of the kingdom of God. Did not my Word say, I will add all things unto you? Indeed, that is what my Word says. I am the living Word. I know my Word, and I know what it means. I honor my Word above my name; that is how significant my Word is. Turn not to the right or the left but keep your focus steadfast on me.

When you tap into my grace and goodness, not of things, but of me having a sincere desire to fellowship and commune with me, you will begin to tap into what true love is. Then you will see that despite all the things you have done to displease me, as soon as you ask for forgiveness and seek my heart and not my hand, I will release them if it is the will of God for you. As soon as you repent, I cast those sins in the sea of forgetfulness and remember them no more. I am not counting your sins; I am asking you to repent of your sins. Be made clean, be made whole in me. How do you make yourself complete in me?

John 15:7 (KJV)

If ye abide in me, and my words abide in you, ye shall ask what ye will, and it shall be done unto you.

When you honor my Word, I will honor you. When you obey my Word, I will bless you. True love, devotion, dedication, and obedience, my child will yield fruit that will always abound to your account. So, you ask me what love is? It is not phileo. True love is obedience, yielding to me, fellowshipping with me, and honoring my Word. I extended myself in love to you, and I desire your love back. The way to get into my heart is by surrendering your heart. I miss you, children. I miss your fellowship. My love for you is from everlasting to everlasting. Come sit at my feet and learn of me, says the Lord.

Prayer

Heavenly Father I want to thank you for demonstrating the ultimate sacrifice of love by sending your son Jesus to die on the cross for me. I am eternally grateful, and I want to say thank you. Help me Holy Spirit to become selfless and to be an example of love to others as it has been extended to me by Jesus. Help me to see through your eyes Lord Jesus and have a synchronized heart that beats to your rhythm. Then and only then, Lord will I truly be able to love unconditionally and share that love with others being a true discipline of your grace in Jesus' name. Amen.

Parable of the Sower

J esus came to the earth and poured out His life for us as a drink offering. He came to serve, not to be served.

Jesus, the living Word, came to teach the kingdom of God and to set an example of how important it is to allow the Word of God to take root in your life. I remember a story in the Bible where people followed Jesus around for hours, even days, to hear His wisdom. He expounded on the Word of God, teaching truths and parables that would confound the wise. Jesus had been teaching by the seaside with his disciples gathered in a boat. The people listened in anticipation as He taught them the parable of the sower.

Mark 4:3-8, (NET)

A sower went out to sow. And as he sowed, some seed fell along the path, and the birds came and devoured it. Other seed fell on rocky ground where it did not have much soil. It sprang up at once because the soil was not deep. When the sun came up it was scorched, and because it did not have sufficient root, it withered. Other seed fell among the thorns, and they grew up and choked it, and it did not produce grain. But other seed fell on good soil and produced grain, sprouting and growing; some yielded thirty times as much, some sixty, and some a hundred times.

Jesus is an all-wise King! Jesus never wasted words and knew how precious His time on earth was. Therefore, He maximized every moment of His time. Although the disciples were with Him and watched Him perform many miracles, they at times did not understand, walked in doubt and unbelief, and lacked faith. So, when they were alone with Jesus, they asked Him to unravel the mystery of the parable.

66

Estella Smith

Mark 4:14-20 (KJV)

The sower sows the word and these are they by the wayside where the word is sown; but when heard, Satan cometh immediately and taketh away the word sown in their hearts. And these are they likewise which are sown on stony ground; who when they have heard the word immediately receive it with gladness and have no root in themselves and so endure but for a time; afterwards when affliction or persecution arises for the words sake, immediately they are offended and these are they which are sown among the thorns, such as hear the word and the cares of this world and the deceitfulness of riches and the lust of other things enter in and choke the word and it becomes unfruitful. And these are they which are sown on good ground, such as hear the word, and receive it, and bring forth fruit, some thirty-fold, sixty-fold and some hundred-fold.

Now, let us take a moment and examine the parable. Where do you see yourself in that parable? Which parable in the Word of God represents your faith level? Let us liken the sower to your pastor when the Word of God goes forth at church, on television, or on social media. When you hear the Word, are you distracted, thinking about what you will cook after church or what pleasure you can indulge in after the service is over? Are you allowing your children to irritate you because they're misbehaving? However, there was an invitation for them to go to the children's church. Are you texting, on social media, or asleep? Maybe, you are disengaged altogether, and you are only showing up for the Word of God because it is an obligation. You have no interest in the Word at all. Is it just the religious thing to do? I have given you examples of scattered seeds sown that produce no harvest in your life. The seeds that the preacher planted fell by the wayside. They hear the Word, and the greed, lust, the eyes of pride of life enter them, and the Word of God is fruitless.

The following parable is when the Word is sowed into the person's heart as they sit in the service. They receive the Word with gladness, take notes, read and study the Word, pray, fast, worship, and praise the Lord. While things are going well in their lives, God is good! But, as soon as a trial or difficult situation arises in their lives, they begin to doubt, complain, or become double-minded. Maybe it is an affliction, or they're offended by someone or something. They do not use the Word as a reference to overcome the testing or trial. Instead, they become faint at heart because something has become too difficult for them to bear. They become frustrated, and their faith begins to falter. Although they were singing praises to their God and reading the Word before, they forget what would sustain them through the sermons they heard previously. The Lord will always give you the tools and resources you need to pass the test before the test comes. We as believers must remember what we did by God's grace to win the previous battle. We must gain the victory and not allow what we are going through to dictate who we are or how the outcome of our lives should be. The Word works instantly, in season and out of season, through the storm, the rain, and the calm.

Now, the final example of the sower is the mature believer who listens to the Word of God, is a student of the Word, prays, fast, and takes notes during sermons. They exemplify 2 Timothy 2:15, (NKJV). It says, "Be diligent to present yourself approved to God, a worker who does not need to be ashamed, rightly dividing the word of truth." The Word is hidden in their heart, and they make application of the Word of God. They seek God for direction and guidance and lean on Holy Spirit to completely take over their lives in the good times and the bad times. They do not falter in their faith. Even if they do, it is only for a moment because they know that the enemy is always watching whom he may devour. They are vigilant in their pursuit of the Lord, and intimacy with the Lord is their mainstay. They realize and know that they would not overcome the enemy if not for the Lord on their side. The mature believer partners with God and does not go before Him. The mature believer allows the Holy Spirit to direct their path. The Holy Spirit is their governance. As long as they stay focused, attentive, and keep the line of communication and relationship open with the Holy Spirit, they win every time, no matter what is happening.

The mature believer can hear a baby crying in church or hear a barrage of thoughts simultaneously that has nothing to do with the sermon going forth. However, they understand that this could be a diversion of the enemy to keep them from hearing the Word of God. Their immediate response is to cast down their vain imaginations and say a prayer quietly under their breath to dismantle the powers of darkness. They will decree in the atmosphere that it will come into alignment with peace and bind the distractions that are going on around them. Yet, maintaining their focus on the Word of God as it is going forth. Satan comes to steal the Word of God at all costs. As a believer, you must be wise to his devices. Mature believers receive manifold blessings because they have learned how to accept and walk in God's grace for each day. "It is not by might or by power but by the Spirit," says the Lord. So, the question is, which of the sowers are you? It is not a question to allow condemnation or judgment to take root. It is simply enlightenment to know your enemy and his tricks, wields, and schemes because he undoubtedly is studying you.

As a mature believer, the Word is necessary meat for you. The Word is tried and true because it has been tested.

Proverbs 4:20-22, (NIV)

My son, pay attention to what I say; turn your ear to my words. Do not let them out of your sight, keep them within your heart; for they are life to those who find them and health to one's whole body.

You must stand on the Word of God being instant in season and out of season, always abounding in the works of the Lord. The goal is to be a believer that is not easily shaken and not so easily moved by one's emotions. We must examine ourselves holistically and stop pretending that we are in some great place in God that we may not be at that moment. Yes, you may have an excellent relationship with Holy Spirit. I am not saying that you do not, but what I am saying is there is always room for improvement. We have been given Holy Spirit as a counselor and helper to lead us in all truth.

Strive to always be transparent with yourself, make the necessary changes, and come into proper alignment with the creator through Holy Spirit. Align and see yourself in the Word of God. You are an ambassador of Jesus Christ on the earth, so when you hear the Word of God, allow it to take root in your heart. You will yield an increase both in the natural and the spiritual. That is what you want as a dual agent. You're a spirit living on earth for this dispensation of time and God's ambassador having a temporary natural experience while being backed by all of heaven and its resources at your disposal.

I talked about the parable of the sower and the need to make sure that the reader is not getting lost in the story without understanding the importance of how the drink offering and the sower marry together. Jesus is the seed or the sower, who sowed Himself for the world. I talked about individuals having different perspectives in handling a given responsibility or assignment. In the scenarios, each individual made choices to increase or decrease the boss's earnings. Your perception, wisdom, and understanding of what has been entrusted to you will determine how or if you multiply, increase or advance in life.

In the parable, one individual did not discern or understand or have enough insight to take the word he heard and capitalize on it to gain increase for his master. The other individual heard the word or instruction he was given and multiplied his master's earnings because he knew his master desired to gain profits. The last individual understood the heart of his master and multiplied his master's earnings and was rewarded for his efforts to please his master. He put his heart into the word that he heard from his master and brought him much gain. The commonalities between the sower and the drink offering are this, the mature sower is the person that hears the Word, applies the Word, and receives the manifestation of the Word because he applies the Word in faith without wavering.

Jesus poured out his life as a drink offering, which means he gave his life for us without hesitation so that we could live an abundant whole life in Him. In turn, just as He surrendered on the cross for you, He expects you to pour your life out for Him and commit your love to Him without fail. You will in turn sow your life to Him unconditionally just as He sowed Himself for you on the cross. This is how the Sower parable and Jesus as a drink offering collide and when you trust Him the two marry as one.

In the beginning, I said that Jesus came as a drink offering for us. He came to pour out His life selflessly to a people that could and would reject Him. He took no thought of His own life, only doing what He saw and heard His Father say and do. That sounds like someone who is surrendered to God the Father.

So, I pose this question to you. Will you accept the challenge to live a life poured out as a drink offering for the Lord Jesus? Will you surrender your will to Him and say, "Not my will King Jesus, but that your perfect will be done on earth as it is in heaven"? Will you say, "I decrease Lord so that you may increase in me. Holy Spirit, please take me over, I surrender all"? Will you receive thirty-fold, sixty-fold, or one hundred-fold in this life and the life to come by yielding your life to God and allowing Holy Spirit to pour the wells of life into you? Will you surrender all to the Lord Christ and not live, then die on full. Will you pour your life out as a drink offering unto the Lord? You decide!

Prayer

Heavenly Father, you sent the Holy Spirit to be the helper, my guide so that I can move, live, and have my being in you. I am your representative, your change agent on the earth because I was bought with the precious blood of Jesus. I am asking for your forgiveness for not allowing the Word of God to take root in my life. I am asking you, Lord, to forgive me for devaluing the Word of God. I will allow the Word of God to change me from the inside out. Please help me, Holy Spirit, to conform to the will of my Heavenly Father so that I am pleasing to Him. I want to live a life that is poured out unto the Lord Jesus. I give you permission Holy Spirit to take me over. I sow my life as a drink offering unto the Lord because He poured out His life for me. Let your kingdom come, Lord Jesus, and your perfect will be done on earth as it is in heaven in my life. In Jesus' name. Amen.

Heaven Bound

Have you taken the time to stop and observe God's creation? The Bible says that God spoke things into existence. Can you imagine the power of those words? As you are going about your day, have you taken the time to look up at the sky to observe the beautiful colors and shapes as they take their unique form? There are times that the sky looks like a perfect painter's canvas with colors streaking throughout. If you have a vivid imagination, you will see rays of light appear from behind the clouds. Is God, the creator of the universe, sending a message of hope, love, and joy to the world?

Let your imagination take you deeper into a realm that far surpasses this earth realm. Let us venture past the clouds, the firmament above the heavens that you can see. We're going past the second heavens where Satan dwells and his principalities and powers rulers of darkness into the third heaven where God the Father and Jesus Christ live. They abide in a magnificent city.

The Word of God says this city has streets made of gold. This immaculate city with crystal clear water, walls made of jasper, and twelve foundations of various stones. I have listened to multiple people giving their accounts on television or in a book of out-of-body encounters they experienced. They had the opportunity to be summoned to heaven by an angel of the Lord or the Lord Jesus Himself.

Let me take this moment to interject something here. I know with so much deception of the enemy, it may seem far-fetched that a human would be able to have such an incredible encounter with the Lord. I will be bold enough to say this. Who are we to take our finite minds and make it resolute as the gospel to say that a person could not have an encounter with God or King Jesus. The

Lord can do whatever He chooses to do. You submit to Him. He does not submit to you. I know that statement may sound harsh, and trust me, I am not trying to sound brash. But, we are serving a God that created the box you are trying to put Him in.

Children of God, we must not make our finite minds the gospel. We cannot put God in a box because it seems unrealistic. I have noticed that some believers have no problem believing what Satan does and think he is powerful. Still, when it comes to the things of God, there is always doubt or reservations. One reservation that a person could have regarding the supernatural and faith is that when we live in a physical world, it is hard to wrap our minds around a world or another dimension that we cannot see. It takes faith to believe in something you cannot see.

There are those who only want to believe in science because they choose to believe in something that connects the dots or in their finite minds has to make sense, or it is not real. If there is not a formula that says how or why something works, or something exists they don't believe it. Science and faith are opposites of other.

Another reason some people have doubts and reservations about God is that they don't understand why as a believer a person can say that God is good and loving but there is death all around us, calamity, poverty, pain, etc. In an unbeliever's eyes, even some believers, don't see how He can be a good God and bad things happen. There is a disconnect when we only look at things from the physical without seeing that there are spiritual aspects and an unseen world around us. God gets a bad rap a lot because He is blamed for anything that's not good in someone's life. There are things that even as a believer you wonder why Lord did this happen. But we need to trust that God has us in the palm of His hands if we have faith to believe He can deliver us from any storm or situation we may face. He only wants the best for us even when tragic things happen in our lives. He may allow things to happen that are painful and detrimental but that doesn't mean that He is the source of the things that happened.

Let's refocus on heaven. John 14:3 (NKJV) says, "And if I go and prepare a place for you, I will come again and receive you to Myself; that where I am, there you may be also." Think about that. God is seated on the throne in Heaven. It is a place of His glory and majesty, and we will be there with Him.

We must not lose sight that the earth is not our home. We are sojourners that are only passing through this temporary place of residence. We are having an earthly experience, but we are spirits that are heavenly bound. Yes, there will be a new heaven and a new earth in the time to come, but we can't negate the fact that we will be with our Heavenly Father as well. Therefore, God wants you to desire the things of the spirit far greater than the things of the world because these things shall pass away.

It is understandable why we do not think about eternal things as much as heaven-bound things because we are in an earthly body. We live on the earth, and our experience is worldly. However, when you are abiding by the Word of God and have an intimate relationship with Holy Spirit, the Spirit will always prompt you to think and live from a spiritual perspective. Your spirit man is whole. Your flesh is not saved and tries to dictate to you how and what you should be doing. As the believer, you have been given dominion over your mind, will, and emotions. They are not subject to you; you subdue them to give glory to God. We can get so caught up being busy with mundane things in our daily lives that we lose sight of who we are and our purpose for being here on the earth. This life is a vapor; it is but for a moment.

It gives Satan such great joy to see God's children taking on the cares of this world through every fiery dart that he throws at you. But, if you cannot discern that they are his missiles, you are stuck longer in the situation than you should be. Colossians 3:1 (KJV) says, "if you were raised with Christ seek those things which are above where Christ is sitting at the right hand of God. Set your mind on things above on things of the earth." Yes, God created the earth for us to enjoy. He gave us family, friends, careers, and vacations to see his incredible creation up close and personal. Yet, these things will pale in comparison to spending all eternity with God and the Lord Jesus Christ. What an honor to know that if we live a Holy life, we will be able to live for all eternity with the Lord Jesus! That is a selah moment! Pause and think of that!

The Bible says that the earth is the Lord's footstool. Children of God, we have dual citizenship. Think about that. We are citizens of another kingdom.

Estella Smith

God sent us to the earth to fulfill our assignment. We are here to live for a destined purpose, and then we are out of here, praise God! Unfortunately, there are too many believers living with a mindset of worldly possessions and things. They are caught up in the vanity of this world, the riches, wealth, clothes, and jewelry. I am not saying that as a believer you cannot have those things, but those things should not have you. The Word of God says in Psalm 24:1 (NEV), "The Lord owns the earth and all it contains, the world and all who live in it." 1 Corinthians 10:26 (TPT), says "for the earth and all its abundance belongs to the Lord."

As children of God, we know that He has called us to steward the land and rule in dominion. If we are called to be kings and priests, we are supposed to walk in great places in God. That includes wealth and riches, but let's keep it real. God said He gives us all things richly to enjoy; therefore, I am not advocating for poverty. I do not believe that God, the creator of all things good, would want to see His children in lack and poverty. I am saying, brothers and sisters, we must examine our hearts and make sure things do not become our God.

The things that the Lord is preparing for us in heaven far exceed the earthly possessions we may acquire. That frame of mind is low thinking if the truth be told. Your relationship with the Lord and honor to Him is far more precious and important than anything you can acquire. When you get God, all those things will be added unto you. So let us set our affections on the things above and not only on the things of the earth. If you think more about earthly things, it can diminish your heavenly mindset. Your focus will be consumed here. Then you are not preparing for the journey home to be with your maker, Heavenly Father, and King Jesus, our Savior.

By no means am I saying do not enjoy earthy things. What I am saying is to enjoy the things He blesses you with because He is the giver of the gifts but seek Him first. That is a higher way of thinking. When you put Him first, He will bless you beyond your wildest dreams on earth, and you are storing up treasures in heaven as well. Think about that! You will receive dual blessings, heavenly and earthly things. Selah! Shift your perspective and live on purpose for Jesus for that eternal weight of glory. Hallelujah!

Prayer

Lord Jesus, thank you for preparing a place for me in heaven. You said that you would come again and receive me unto yourself. I repent for thinking more about this earthly world than setting my mind on things heaven-bound. Instead, I should have prepared my heart to receive you while fulfilling my assignment on earth. Then when I pass from death to eternal life, I will be with you forever in heaven in glory. The first step is to ask you to forgive me of my sins Lord, sins of omission and commission, and cleanse me from all unrighteousness. I repent and turn away from my sins and receive you as my Lord and my Savior Lord Jesus Christ. Amen.

Wisdom of God

How often have we thought we had it all together only to find out that the sensual wisdom of the world is flawed and considered foolishness to God?

You can have a doctorate or higher education, achieve great things in your career, and have a loving family with a white picket fence. It looks good to the world and on paper, very polished, and picture-perfect to some, but God does not look at the outward appearance. He looks at the heart.

1 Corinthians 3:18-19, (NKJV)

Let no man deceive himself. If any man among you seems to be wise in this world, let him become a fool, that he may become wise. For the wisdom of this world is foolishness to God. For it is written, "He catches the wise in their craftiness"

There are professional students and people who are constantly seeking the next great thing; going to the latest conference, getting the next degree, or getting another certification. They have a quest for knowledge, and there is nothing wrong with that. I, too, have degrees, but if you are continually seeking knowledge without wisdom that comes from the Holy Spirit, all you have is knowledge. I am not speaking about the world's wisdom, but the wisdom of God, which comes from an eternal place.

1 Corinthians 2:5 (NLV) In this way, you do not have faith in Christ because of the wisdom of men. You have faith in Christ because of the power of God.

The Word of God says that knowledge can puff you up if not appropriated correctly. Seeking wisdom from a natural or humanistic perspective is a lesser intelligence. It will not carry the glory and backing of God with it. You want the weight in the spirit, the support of the Holy Spirit; He is the seal of promise.

Some great leaders, and scholars, have seen many things transpire in their life walk in wisdom. Books have been written full of wisdom where someone talks about lessons learned through their experiences. Take that wisdom and use it for your life if it is not compromising your walk in the Lord. Although those forms of knowledge can be good reference points, when you compare that to the infinite wisdom of God, there is none to be compared to Him, the wisdom of ages.

I've heard people say, "Experience is the best teacher." Let us look into this statement a little deeper. Why would you want to make unnecessary mistakes and experience setbacks and delays because of your choices? Then state that experience is the best teacher. When you believe in Jesus Christ and have the Holy Spirit living inside of you, He will lead and guide your every movement if you allow Him to. Therefore, experience should not be the best teacher. Holy Spirit is the voice of wisdom and is the best teacher. He will show you all things that are to come. He sees, hears, and knows all things because He is in tune with the mind of the Father. Now that is a wisdom statement you can make applicable to your life.

The Lord will allow you to go through difficult and very trying situations to develop your faith, to bring you closer to Him. Please make sure that you heard that sentence correctly. I said that He would allow you to go through things. I did not say that He tempts you to sin. Satan is the accuser of the brethren that throws spiritual assaults and arrows at you in hopes that you will lose faith in God during your trials and abort the process Holy Spirit will do in you throughout difficult times if you allow Him to. Walking in the wisdom of God is to explicitly obey the voice of the Holy Spirit always.

Proverbs 16:25 (KJV) says, "there is a way that seems right to man, but the end thereof are the ways of death." We go through things God does not ordain because we did not seek Him for instruction and wise counsel. As a result, we can stay in a situation longer than intended, like the children of Israel wandering around in the wilderness for 40 years when it should have only taken 11 days to complete the journey.

Proverbs 1:5 (KJV) says, "a wise man will hear and will increase in learning and a man of understanding shall attain wise counsel." God in His sovereignty, the wisdom of days, knows all things. He is a loving Father who is waiting on you to commune with Him. His infinite wisdom will never run out. So, create room for Him in your life each day. Talk to Him. Tell Him what is on your mind and in your heart. I promise you, it will not catch Him by surprise.

When you receive the wisdom from the Father, think about it. His wisdom comes from a pure source that has never sinned, never had a wrong thought. Everything that He says, does, and decides comes from a pure place with no hidden agendas. He loves His creation and only has the best intentions for us all, whether we serve Him or not. Therefore, He is uninhibited by selfish desires. This pure wisdom breaks yokes, destroys burdens, brings deliverance, has the ability and power to change your season, knows how to overturn the accusations of Satan, and brings healing to His people. There is no dynamic that the Lord's wisdom cannot penetrate. We base earthly wisdom on book knowledge, life experiences, and man's opinion.

Proverbs 2:2-5 (TPT)

So train your heart to listen when I speak and open your spirit wide to expand your discernment—then pass it on to your sons and daughters. Yes, cry out for comprehension and intercede for insight. For if you keep seeking it like a man would seek for sterling silver, searching in hidden places for cherished treasure, then you will discover the fear of the Lord and find the true knowledge of God.

The Lord wants us to be willing to receive Him and His Word because His Word produces life in us. However, He also wants you to hide the Word in your heart because there will come a day when you are tested on the Word or instruction you heard. God's ways are higher than our ways, and His thoughts are higher than our thoughts. Therefore, as believers in Jesus Christ, we must put on the mind of Christ Jesus and take the high road, wisdom, which is the principal thing.

Prayer

Heavenly Father, I repent for trying to pretend that I have it all together and can handle the affairs of life without your help. I repent for not acknowledging you first and seeking the kingdom of God, and allowing all things to be added unto me. I ask you to lead me in the way I should go and guide me with your wisdom. I submit to the leading of the Holy Spirit's wisdom and direction for my life because His way is perfect. I will trust in you with all my heart and lean not to my understanding, and in all my ways, I will acknowledge you and allow you to direct my path. In Jesus' name. Amen.

Mirror Me

There are billions of people on this planet, and Heavenly Father uniquely creates everyone. Your DNA is designed specifically for you. He spoke who you were to be into your spirit and put purpose in you. Your facial appearance is unlike anyone else's on this planet. Even if you are an identical twin and look exactly like your sibling, your DNA makes you stand apart in your God-given uniqueness.

Have you ever felt like you were alone, even in a room full of people? Maybe there is someone in your circle of friends or a family member who is always getting into trouble and has a less desirable reputation than everyone else. As a result, they are considered the outcast of the group. Have you or someone you know felt that no matter how hard you try, you just do not fit anywhere you go? As a result, you feel like a third wheel, or you get wrongfully judged by others because they sense that you are different.

Hebrews 4:16 (TPT)

So now we draw near freely and boldly to where grace is enthroned, to receive mercy's kiss and discover the grace we urgently need to strengthen us in our time of weakness.

The enemy will allow these negative emotions to plague you and make you feel like you are less than someone else or send negative arrows or words into your soul. You begin to think that you are not good enough. If you have a poor self-image, he will try to keep you isolated so that he can continue to take you down a downward spiral. If you don't get around positive influences, read the Word, and say, "I am not who the people say I am," you will believe someone else's perspective of you. The enemy wants you to become withdrawn and passive. That can lead to you becoming melancholy and falling into the enemy's clutches because you submitted to his devices. Ecclesiastes 4:9-10 New Living Translation (NLT) says, "Two people are better off than one, for they can help each other succeed. If one person falls, the other can reach out and help. But someone who falls alone is in real trouble."

God did not create clones. Instead, He made unique individuals with personalities shaped by circumstances and life experiences. Unfortunately, in society, people can be cruel and judgmental. As a result, they may cause you to be ostracized, criticized, and even rejected because you do not act, look, dress, or live a certain way.

If you are a born-again believer in Jesus Christ, God calls you chosen. You are a royal priesthood, a holy nation. God has picked you out. Let's pause and think of that. God handpicked you. The Word tells us many are called, but few are chosen. Why is that, you may ask? Because many will reject the Lord Jesus Christ when He calls them. When God chooses you, it is an unconditional election.

Deuteronomy 14:2, (NIV)

for you are a people holy to the LORD your God.

Out of all the peoples on earth, the LORD chose you to be His treasured possession. Let us tie all these thoughts together. Someone thinks that you are a troublemaker based on your actions or deeds. They may judge you based on your past. Although you have put that behind you and moved forward, some people will still choose to see you from their perspective. Do not accept the lies of the enemy. Whether you are a born-again believer or not, please do not allow anyone to make you feel as though you are not good enough.

Do not allow naysayers to dictate who you are or what you will become? Whether you are a born-again believer or not, God created you, and there is no one like you. He broke the mold when He made you. Now, you need to believe that about yourself. Get in the Word of God and see what He says about you and who you are to Him. Keep your focus and surroundings on positive things, things that lift you, not tear you down.

As a believer, you changed from the kingdom of darkness into light and danced with a new partner. God calls you holy, righteous, and peculiar unto Himself. He says that you are the apple of His eye, you are the elect of God, and you cannot get any better than this. So stop where you are and give God praise. Hallelujah!

If you are not born again or have not accepted Jesus Christ as your Lord and personal savior, it can be the best choice you could make. However, it is not my assignment to persuade an unbeliever by going against his or her will. I will share this based on my decision to accept Jesus as my Lord and Savior.

The Word of God says that Jesus died on the cross for the sins of the world. He loved the people of the world so much that regardless of what sins we have committed now or in our past, He will forgive us of our sins when we confess the sins to Him, and He will cleanse us of all unrighteousness. In other words, He will forgive us for anything and everything we ever did. The Lord wants us to yield to Him so He can lead us on a plain path of a life that is not broken, but whole in Him when we trust Him. Jesus wants to saturate you in His unconditional love without condemning you of your faults. But, lovingly walking you through the transformation to truly fulfilling love that no earthly person can give you.

The unmeasurable love of God and the Holy Spirit is the only way a person can receive Christ Jesus as their Savior. If you still have reservations, I challenge you to have an open conversation with Jesus and ask Him if He is real. Ask Him to reveal Himself to you. What do you have to lose? You may be surprised by the results. I challenge you to consider what the Word of God says about you being the head and not the tail, above only, never beneath. If you are not ready to make Jesus Christ your Savior, find positive affirmations and speak them over yourself. Fortify yourself with all things positive to help build your spirit so that you can stand against every lie of the devil.

Arise from the ashes, arise, child of God. There is no one like you. You are an original. Do not think ground level; you are not the base of anything. You are seated in heavenly places in Christ Jesus far above all principalities, and powers, might, and dominion. In the kingdom of God, you go down to come up. In the world, they see things from the outside, then within. The only time you are basic with God is when you are walking lowly before the Father. You walk in humility, allowing your flesh to be processed so that you can reign in victory, triumph, favor, righteousness, and glory. It has nothing to do with feeling inferior or beneath. It means that you submitted to the Lord Christ and yield to obey His leading and instructions through the Holy Spirit.

If someone tries to make you feel beneath them, like you do not fit in their circles of influence or with a particular group, dismiss it and reject the enemy's lies. Open your eyes to see that if you are God's chosen, He does not want you belittled by someone that does not walk in His character. He lives inside of you. So, to you, I say, come up higher in your thinking. God created you to be unique, and His love is a judgment-free zone. If He does not treat you in disrespectful ways, do not allow others to treat you that way. You do not deserve that.

Prayer

Heavenly Father, I thank you that I have been seated in heavenly places with you. I thank you that I am chosen and set apart by you as the elect of God. I will renew my mind in the Word of God so that when the enemy shoots his arrows, they will not penetrate my soul. I have on the shield of faith to quench every fiery dart of the enemy. I am who you say that I am, and I thank you for choosing me. No matter what man thinks about me, I chose life and surround myself with people who love me unconditionally. They accept me the way I am because you accept me. I will allow the Word of God to change me into your image and likeness and will walk in the fullness of joy. In Jesus' name. Amen.

Change Your Perception

Life can interrupt you with so many distractions. You can make many plans, five, ten, and twenty-year goals with the high expectation that they will materialize or come to pass. But in a moment, those dreams and desires are shattered by some unforeseen circumstances or situations that you could never have imagined or seen coming. Life's obstacles blindsided you. You may have even checked out of life depending on the severity of the situation. Some never recover from it.

Have you ever watched a storm brewing and the clouds became very dark, covering the skies, and the rain begins to pour down shortly afterward? Then before you know it, there is no sign of light in the skies because the darkness has enveloped the skies. But wait, look again. The sun is piercing through the darkness, and the dark clouds begin to fade away slowly. The sun pierces through the clouds, beaming like the glory of God in its dominance, and the rays of sunlight bring forth light and radiant colors in the sky. Child of God, no matter what obstacles come your way, remember there is always light. So, in the darkness, say, "Father in the name of Jesus, let there be light in Jesus' name!"

I am sure some of you may have heard someone speaking of the hourglass and asked you your view of it. They may ask, "Do you see the hourglass half empty or half full?" There is no right or wrong way to answer the question. It is all based on your perception. What is perception? It is the ability to see, hear, or become aware of something through the senses. It is viewed from the eyes of the beholder.

Let us review the previous scenario regarding the dark clouds that covered the skies. The clouds could represent or symbolize temporary setbacks that can be an opportunity for you to make necessary growth or faith adjustments in your life. The rain that came during the storm could represent cleansing and purging you of your hidden agendas, desires, will, rebellion, disobedience, pride, and emotional ways that displease him. The Lord is cleansing your heart from this present darkness and making all things new.

The part in the analogy where the sun burst through the clouds and dispelled the darkness can be an example of where you are coming out of the darkness into God's marvelous light. You are divinely reset.

Although the enemy has tried to sabotage your life by causing failure, God looks from eternity and sees every plot, plan, scheme, wiles, and trick of the enemy. However, He has a way of escape for you when you stay connected to the vine. John 15:5 (TPT) says, "I am the sprouting vine and you're my branches. As you live in union with me as your source, fruitfulness will stream from within you—but when you live separated from me, you are powerless."

How do you see what you are going through? Is it half empty or half full? Do you stop, re-evaluate your situation and say, Lord, what are you trying to show me that I can learn from and use for your glory? Or are you the person who becomes angry and bitter because you are going through something yet again? Do you wonder when you're going to get me out of the situation and declare, "I am tired of this?" God always comes through for you at the right moment in time. He brings clarity, wisdom, understanding, insight, and strength so that you can endure and weather any storm. Anything that the enemy throws at you, the Word of God will give you the faith muscles you need to exercise your dominion over it if you allow Holy Spirit to work in you and through you.

Colossians 1:11 (TPT)

And we pray that you would be energized with all his explosive power from the realm of his magnificent glory, filling you with great hope.

Your hope is secure when it is found on the solid rock Jesus. Do not trust your intuition, your wisdom, and understanding in all matters without consulting Holy Spirit for guidance and direction. When you embrace the way that you were truly supposed to walk, live, and have your being in Christ without reservations, you will be able to enjoy the benefits of salvation. You will change your perspective on how you see yourself in the natural and in the spirit. Your perception of living will evolve to a higher standing of living because the greater one, Holy Spirit lives inside of you.

Colossians 1:18 (NLT)

Christ is also the head of the church, which is his body. He is the beginning, supreme over all who rise from the dead. So he is first in everything.

Prayer

Lord, I thank you that through your Word and the sweet communion of the Holy Spirit I have been given the grace to see you through the eyes of the spirit. I do not have to settle for mere natural sight or insight that is limited and fragmented. I ask you Holy Spirit to infuse me with your insight and perception of all things. Please open the lens of my eyes in the spirit to clearly see everything you want me to see from your perception and take authority over everything that will oppose your will for my life in Jesus' name. I take on the mindset of Jesus Christ and bring everything that has been set up as a snare to me to become subject to me in Jesus' name. Lord, you are the light that shines in the darkness, and that light cannot be hidden. I stand in the authority of Jesus and command darkness to flee in the name of Jesus Christ. I stand in my authority and command "Light Be" in every area of my life now in Jesus' name. Amen.

Faith and Waiting

ave you ever found yourself whispering, "God, where are you? Lord help me, I need you!" When we are going through trying times, we call on God and expect Him to be right there to take us out of our troubles immediately. We want Him to be our deliverer, the right now God at our every beck and call.

But before the breakthrough, there is a battle. The enemy is always trying to keep you distracted, busy, frustrated, weary, and even in fear so that you will not receive your miracle or breakthrough.

Isaiah 40:31, (NKJV)

But those who wait on the Lord Shall renew their strength; They shall mount up with wings like eagles, They shall run and not be weary, They shall walk and not faint.

God has scheduled a divine time for your breakthrough, your healing, and your deliverance, but you must stand in faith and believe that He will do it. James 1:3 (NLT) says, "For you know that when your faith is tested, your endurance has a chance to grow." There is a place and stance that you can take in God to put such a demand on your faith that God will respond sooner than expected. You must have tenacity, unwavering faith, the kind of faith that says, "I shall not be moved. This is my inheritance, and I will receive the end of my faith." The kind of faith where you are rock steady in God. The enemy wants you to doubt and think that God does not love you or that He does not hear your prayers. When you know that the enemy is attacking you on every side, that is not the time to cower away and hide. God has given you the authority to speak to the mountain and tell it to move in Jesus' name.

There are times when you may be fighting God and do not know it. An example of this could be when He has given you instruction. It is not that you won't do it, but you are doing it in a different way than He told you to do it, although you may arrive at the same result. You may be asking God to do something for you or someone you know, but it is not His will for you to receive your request. Maybe it's not the right season for it. God is more interested in purifying and purging your heart than your prayer request. He is looking at your motives as to why you want something. Is it for your selfish gain, or is it a blessing to yourself and others in the Kingdom? Is it for His glory?

When the enemy sees that your relationship with the Lord Christ is consistent and you are in the presence of the Lord seeking him with your whole heart, He intervenes with fiery darts, chaos, calamity, sickness, depression, oppression, etc. The goal of the enemy is to derail your plans from ever materializing. Therefore, do not allow your problems to dictate to you how you are going to feel. Instead, you tell the problems how big your God is. Jeremiah 29:11 (NIV) says, "For I know the plans I have for you," declares the Lord, "plans to prosper you and not to harm you, plans to give you hope and a future." Hallelujah! You are suited up, praise God!

Failure is not an option. Praise until something happens. Begin to thank God for the things that you cannot see in the natural. He has given you grace for purpose. Grace is something that you do not deserve. You were built for adversity. You were built to weather the storm. You have the greater one living inside of you. You must live by the Word and become a living epistle of the Word of God. Stand, I say, stand in faith, and you will see the promise.

Be persistent in God, do not lose heart, cave in, or quit. Instead, pray with faith and confidence and diligently seek the Lord.

Psalm 130:5 (NET)

I rely on the Lord. I rely on him with my whole being; I wait for his assuring word. It is a sure indication that you are not in control.

Waiting can be painful at times. Waiting takes you out of your need to control and walk in dominance based on your will. It is sometimes impossible to change your circumstances immediately, but they who wait on the Lord shall renew their strength like the eagle. The Word of God says according to Hebrews 10:38, "Now the just shall live by faith and if any man draws back my soul shall have no pleasure in him."

Ephesians 3:20 (TPT)

Never doubt God's mighty power to work in you and accomplish all this. He will achieve infinitely more than your greatest request, your most unbelievable dream, and exceed your wildest imagination! He will outdo them all, for his miraculous power constantly energizes you.

While you are waiting in faith to manifest your desire, be sure to wait with expectation. Your attitude while you are waiting, will determine your altitude. Likewise, your attitude will determine how long you wait.

While you are in the waiting season, watch what is coming out of your mouth. Do not quit, nor walk in the natural at this time. Instead, make sure that you spend quality time with the Lord because you want to hear His instructions. Do not exalt what you are waiting for. Instead, exalt the one you are waiting on, Jesus. Do not allow the enemy to inject doubt and unbelief into your head and complain about why you have not seen the manifestation of your promise. Doubt is the enemy of faith!

A season of expectation is a season of pregnancy. You will give birth to what you believe God for. Stay in faith! Do not have a stillborn. You must go through labor and delivery. If you are on and off in your faith, you will not receive the promise.

When a woman is carrying a child, throughout that pregnancy, she may experience Braxton Hicks. The pains are temporary, but they are not the true contractions that lead to childbirth. The closer the labor pains are coming during your waiting season, the closer your manifestation. You may be getting an intensification of attacks by the enemy so that you may abort the child you are carrying in the spirit.

Romans 10:17 (NKJV)

So then faith comes by hearing, and hearing by the word of God.

I want to give you an example of when I had to stand in faith for something that caused me to really stand on the Word of God and put into practice the teachings I heard. I was laid off from my job and had saved money for emergency purposes. I knew this was one of them. I was drawing unemployment, but my unemployment ran out. I could feel the intensity of the situation because I had a mortgage and bills that needed to be paid and my savings was almost tapped out. I was frustrated because I had put in so many applications for employment but was not getting many calls. The ones that I was getting, the pay was too low, and I was turning down the offers.

At the time when I was turning down the offers, I still had money in the bank, so I knew that this was giving me leverage and buying time. As time progressed, and the money began to get really low. I could feel the anxiety and tension, and my faith started wavering. I had thoughts of losing my home. I would cast down the negative thoughts and continue to speak the Word of God, but I tell you, there were times I didn't know if my faith was going to withstand the pressure.

I was turning down jobs but really had no money. I would read the Word of God stand on His Word, worship, praise, and still feel distracted by the weight of the situation. There were times I felt like I was going to just take the next opportunity that was presented to me because I felt like and heard myself saying these words when I was beginning to waver in my faith, "God you are taking too long and I feel you are not hearing me." I would go back to the scripture Romans 10:17 faith comes by hearing and hearing by the Word of God. I will never forget I was sitting at my computer looking for jobs and I remember saying, I am standing on your Word God, and I will not be disappointed. I shall receive the end of my faith in Jesus' name. I am asking you for a certain amount of money and I am expecting to get it. I will not continue to settle for less and I am a giver. I remember receiving a call from a recruiter offering me a job making more money than I had ever made, praise God. There were some challenging times and wavering faith, but when I continued to apply the Word of God under pressure Jesus manifested Himself to me as my provider, Jehovah Jireh. I give Him all the praise and glory for that.

You must only speak the Word. No matter what it looks like in the waiting season, you must go through the process while standing in faith. The longer the labor, the greater the reward! In the natural, when the baby's head is crowning, and the doctor says push, you feel that you have no strength to push again. But when that child comes out of the birth canal crying, and she sees the wonder of God's creation, the mother forgets the pain and suffering during the nine-month process. Everything that she went through was worth the wait. So likewise, you may have wanted to give up and say God is not going to do this for me or this is taking too long, but when you see the manifestation of your dream or desire, it will be well worth the faith muscles that you built during the process. Corinthians 4:17 (KJV) says, "For our light affliction, which is but for a moment, worketh for us a far more exceeding and eternal weight of glory." Glory to God!

Prayer

Lord Jesus, I know that there are times when I have doubted you and your Word and have delayed the manifestation of your promises. Therefore, I repent and ask you to forgive me. Your Word says it is impossible to please you without faith, so help me, Holy Spirit, to be a person that lives by faith. I am the seed of Abraham, and I shall inherit my promises when I stand firm in the faith, giving glory to God without wavering. In Jesus' name. Amen.

Faith Walker

As I pondered on the children of Israel in the Old Testament, I thought about the sheer mercy of God. Many notable miracles took place in the Old Testament, where God made Himself known to the children of Israel and demonstrated His character and attributes to them. One of the notable signs of God's authority and power was when He parted the Red Sea for the children of Israel as He led them out of bondage from Pharaoh, king of Egypt. Moses was given an assignment by God to deliver the children of Israel out of four hundred years of bondage and slavery under Pharoah. Moses led the children of Israel into the wilderness on an unprecedented journey. God showed Himself strong on their behalf and was described as the great "I AM." Jehovah caused Pharaoh to lose his hold on the children of Israel by hardening his heart and bringing various plagues upon the land due to his harsh treatment of the children of Israel. Pharaoh was so worn out by the plagues that he abruptly told Moses to take the children of Israel and leave Egypt. Not only did the children of Israel leave a life of slavery, but they left Egypt with gold, silver, and the possessions of their enemies. Praise God, they left with the spoils! Isaiah 45:3 (NIV) says, "I will give you hidden treasures, riches stored in secret places, so that you may know that I am the LORD, the God of Israel, who summons you by name." Isn't that just like God to position His people to take the spoils from our enemies and give them to His elect?

When Pharaoh realized that He had given Moses His laborers and possessions, he became outraged and sent his army after them. Moses had come to what would look like the end of the road for him and the millions of Israelites God had entrusted to him. He knew that he could do nothing but trust in the Lord for direction and instruction. I can imagine Moses' conversation with God went something like this: "Now, God, I was minding my own business tending to my sheep on the backside of the mountain, when the angel of the Lord appeared to me and said, you called me out at Mount Horeb. I saw the burning bush, and you began to speak to me about the oppression of your people and how you heard their cries and wanted to deliver them from Egypt out of the hands of Pharaoh." He looks at the sea before him and his enemies in hot pursuit behind him. Moses hears the people crying out to him. They could hear the horse and chariots coming behind them, sounding like an earthquake as the horse's huffs hit the ground in unison, drawing closer and closer to the children of Israel standing by the sea.

The cries of the children of Israel and complaining about how they felt they would be slaughtered by Pharaoh's army by the sea quickly brought Moses back into focus. Moses thinks about the promise that God made to him. God told Moses He would be with him wherever he went.

Moses snapped out of the momentary disillusionment and said, "Okay, I trust you, God. You didn't bring me this far to leave me." As soon as Moses refocused, took his mind off the present situation, and put his mind back on almighty God, he assumed a different posture and position. He was the Prophet of the Lord. I am sure Moses took a moment to reflect on all the things he saw God do concerning the plagues in Egypt. That reminder assured Moses that this was not an assignment he chose, but it was a mandate from God. Moses knows that he had to trust God with this assignment because it was bigger than him, and after all, these were not his people. These were God's people. After that, I am sure that Moses had an epiphany of the unfailing love of God and His faithfulness to His Word.

Philippians 4:19 (AMP)

And my God will liberally supply (fill until full) your every need according to His riches in glory in Christ Jesus.

Moses knew that he could do nothing outside of God. He looked at the Red Sea and Pharaoh's army fast on their heels with nowhere to go. Jehovah God told Moses to take the staff in his hands and point it towards the ocean by faith. The God of Israel parted the Red Sea so the children of Israel could cross over to the other side on dry ground. When the children of Israel crossed over on the dry land, the waters held upwards by the word of God's power resumed their position, and Pharoah's army was consumed by the massive water and drowned. Psalm 78:53 (NIV) tells us, "He guided them safely, so they were unafraid; but the sea engulfed their enemies." The children of Israel saw another dimension and revelation of God's power and knew Him as God Omnipotent.

The children of Israel continued in their wilderness journey experience and saw the mighty hand of God move on their behalf in significant ways. The God of Israel fed the children of Israel, and they had no wants or needs. The Bible says in Psalm 105:37 (KJV), "He brought them forth also with silver and gold: and there was not one feeble person among their tribes." The Lord God was their cloud by day and a pillar of fire by night. They knew Him as their protection and guiding light.

The children of Israel had many obstacles and wars to fight on their way to the promised land. If they adhered to the God-given instructions of Moses, the Lord's hand was with them in the battles, and they would win every one. However, sometimes they chose to disobey the instructions. Examples of this were when they were marrying outside of their tribe, worshipping other gods, and not obeying the voice of God. They would lose battles, be judged, and be captured by their enemies because the Lord was not with them. Yet, they continued to rebel and serve other idols. God would correct and bring judgment based on their decisions.

We can look at the children of Israel's narratives and say how could they do this and that when they saw all the notable miracles, signs, and wonders God performed before their very eyes. But, before we cast that stone, how many times has God given us a directive, and we disobeyed? How often have we completed a partial instruction from the Lord and thought that we had arrived when we compared ourselves in our self-righteousness to someone who had not finished or even started an assignment from the Lord? So, of the two, who do you think is in better standing with the Lord? Let me help you. The answer is neither because if you don't complete the Lord's instructions, whether you disobeyed by doing nothing or started an assignment but did not complete it, you are judged on the same scale. Either you complete the task, or you do not. Delayed and partial obedience is still disobedience in the eyes of God. He wants your "yes" in its totality.

Now, let us go back to the children of Israel for a moment. God did not send Moses to be a deliverer of His chosen elect to flex His muscles and demonstrate His power. God heard the cry of the children of Israel because they were in bondage to a King that did not know their God nor serve their God. They were in bondage because of their rebellion and continual disobedience to serve other gods. He allowed them to be in captivity for all those years and had mercy on them to deliver them at a set time.

There was a reward for them serving the true and living God. It was the land that flows with milk and honey, the land of Goshen. Let us put a pause on this statement for a moment. How many of us know that God can show or give you a promise but does not tell you how you will receive the manifestation of that promise? He will hook you with a "Word." The Word could be very enticing, and it is typically greater than you so that you will depend on the Lord throughout the process until you see the manifestation of the Word.

You may go through valley and desert experiences in your life and your walk with God just like the children of Israel, but do not shrink back and get upset or quit God because you are overwhelmed with a situation or circumstance.

Isaiah 40:31 (NLT)

But those who trust in the LORD will find new strength. They will soar high on wings like eagles. They will run and not grow weary. They will walk and not faint.

If we are honest with ourselves, would we seek God or pray if we always had it together? He causes things to happen in our lives that drive us into His presence, to commune with Him in prayer, worship, and praise. The children of Israel wandered around in the wilderness for 40 years when it should have only taken them an 11 days journey because of doubt, unbelief, murmuring, complaining, disobedience, doublemindedness, and fear. Do these sound-like attributes of God? Certainly not! Let us take the question a step further. Does any of this sound like your journey in God? Selah!

If the children of Israel were in the spirit instead of the flesh, the narrative would have been different. It could have looked something like this: "Lord, I speak to every mountain in my life, and I command it removed because I trust in you and the voice and instructions of the prophet you have sent to us. We will partner with the living God because we have seen the hand of the Lord walking with us in triumph and victory during difficult times while at war with our enemies, causing us to subdue, plumage, and recover all from our enemies. We have come to know you as Jehovah Gabor, the God of war, and we trust you in every area of our lives. We will not partake of foreign Gods that displease you, which in turn brings judgment upon our heads. We trust you, God, because you have demonstrated your faithfulness to us time and time again."

Isaiah 59:19, (KJV)

So shall they fear the name of the Lord from the west, and his glory from the rising of the sun. When the enemy shall come in like a flood, the Spirit of the Lord shall lift up a standard against him.

Psalm 91:7 (NIV)

A thousand may fall at your side, ten thousand at your right hand, but it will not come near you.

Hallelujah! Ponder this thought. The children of Israel had a leader appointed to them by God, Moses! Moses walked a supernatural life with God. He had an intimate relationship with God put on display so they could see it. God trusted Moses to shepherd millions of people under his direction. Moses wrote by the voice of God the ten commandments, spending intimate time with God in the high places, having mountain top experiences, and glory encounters with God.

God always wants to elevate us to go higher in Him, expand our thinking, and expand our capacity to receive more of Him. We are called to be seated in heavenly places in Christ Jesus, the head and not the tail, above only and not beneath. He called us to be the salt and light in the earth. He set leaders on the earth after His heart to teach and equip His children to walk like Him, talk like Him, believe like Him, carry the glory like Him, and perform signs, wonders, and miracles like Him. We are, as believers, to live in the supernatural daily. This should not be an occurrence or an event but a lifestyle.

The children of Israel saw the miracles, signs, and wonders, and even walked with God as He covered and protected them. Moses spent such a glorious time with God in intimacy that his face shined with glory, and the children of Israel experienced this but were afraid. The children of Israel had that kind of access to a glory carrier like Moses and God himself through the ark of the covenant, and yet they still were more comfortable with sinning, rebelling, and disobeying God. There must have been a disconnect between the children of Israel and Moses regarding having a solid connection and personal relationship with the God of Israel themselves.

When reading the book of Exodus, I would often wonder if the children of Israel discerned who this prophet was in their midst? Or did they become so comfortable with him that they took him for granted? Before you start throwing stones at the children of Israel, how many times have we had the opportunity to serve or work with someone that God called us to submit to, and soon as you were given a task you did not like or agree with, you copped an attitude and said, "Who do they think they are?"

Proverbs 9:10 (NLT), the Word of God says, "Fear of the LORD is the foundation of wisdom. Knowledge of the Holy One results in good judgment." The children of Israel feared the Lord from a soul perspective, but not a reverential fear of the Lord. Do not get it twisted, we have all been in this position at some point in time when we did not know any better. God has shown His hand strong in our lives, and we still doubted him. He has covered us in our mess so that we were not exposed and brought to an open shame in public or before man. What an incredibly loving God with so much mercy for

His children and those who do not serve Him. His love and compassion are from everlasting to everlasting; He is God, and there is none like Him.

God leveled the playing field for everyone. Either you choose to serve and obey him, or you don't and receive the consequences of your choice. He will give each of us instructions that we may or may not agree with or like, but it is up to us to adhere to them or not. He will never force us. Instead, He has given us an example from His Word, which I would like to compare to "SAR," an interviewing technique that some financial institutions use to fill job positions.

During the interview process, your responses must include a Situation, Action, and a Result (SAR) related to that question to see how you react to a given situation or circumstance. For example, if they are looking to see if you are a team player, they may say, tell me about a time that you had to handle conflict on your job". This is your opportunity to expound on a scenario in reference to the question you were asked. After you explain the situation, you will next explain the action(s) that transpired in the situation regarding you and the teammate(s) and follow that up with what the solution was to resolve the issue. This is how a SAR behavioral interview style of questions is conducted by managers at some employers. Our heavenly Father has a manual for you to read and study, which is the Word of God. The spiritual SAR could look something like this, In the Word of God are **Situations** (directions given by God) or situations we may find ourselves in at times called life. **Actions**, (the response of the person to whom the directive was given or the situation that transpired), and the **Result**, the outcome of the action, whether good or bad based on the person's choices.

An example of a spiritual SAR could look something like this: Jesus had performed several miracles and would draw large crowds of people because His fame had increased in various regions. The **situation** would be something like this. Jesus pulled His disciples aside privately because He had performed many miracles but when the multitude of people caught wind of it they began to follow Him wherever He went. Jesus understood that the people were hungry for the Word of God and His wisdom and love for the Father's people lead Him to always walk in compassion and passionate desire to teach all who would listen. The disciples were asking Jesus to tell the crowd of people to go away so that they and Jesus could go into a neighboring town to find lodging and provisions because they were in a desert area. But Jesus told the disciples to get the multitude something to eat, and the disciples responded by telling Jesus that they only have two fish and five loaves. Next is the spiritual **action** (here is the directive) Jesus gave the disciples specific instructions to have the people sit down in groups of fifty then Jesus took the two fish and five loaves and put His faith in motion by looking to His Heavenly Father and Him to multiple the food to feed the multitude. Jesus, the Word of God, did not wave nor stagger in unbelief. He prayed and believed that God would honor His prayer, and the miracle happened before the eyes of everyone present. The spiritual **result** is that everyone ate their food in amazement of the notable miracle performed and there were twelve baskets of food leftover after feeding five thousand people.

Let me give you another example of the spiritual situation, action, and result (SAR). Here is the **situation**. I was given a prophecy by a neighbor that I would write books many years ago, but I did not act on the word that I heard. Jeremiah 30: 2 (NKJV) says, "Thus speaks the Lord God of Israel, saying: 'Write in a book for yourself all the words that I have spoken to you.'" I had not known a prophet before, nor had I met one because I was unfamiliar with the fivefold ministry at that time. I had no idea that I was in direct disobedience for not responding to the word of the Lord. I took it lightly and dismissed it because I couldn't comprehend me writing a book although I used to write a lot when I was younger. It was my personal journaling that I really didn't think much about. It was an escape for me, a way to exhale for a moment from things that I had been experiencing as a teenager into my twenties. I had let insecurities stand in my way and quite honestly, I didn't understand what I was supposed to write a book about. I was looking at everything from the natural senses because I had no knowledge or insight to seek God because I was a baby Christian coming out of a religious church that did not speak on faith, healing, miracles, etc. nor much of the Word of God to be honest.

Action, now fast forward to the year 2020. I remember during Covid 19 I would hear the Lord speaking to me and I would write the things that I heard, not realizing that I was writing the book that you are now reading. Psalm 45:1

(AMP) says, "My heart overflows with a good theme; I address my psalm to the King. My tongue is like the pen of a skillful writer." Once I realized that this was actually the manifestation of the prophecy from many years ago, I had to get in the Word of God and meditate on the Word so that my flesh would not be writing this book. I knew that I needed to decrease so that Christ could increase in me. I would practice sitting in the presence of God so that I could hear Holy Spirit when he began to speak to me because I knew and understood that the Word of the Lord was proceeding out of me, and I dare not fail the Lord this time in disobedience. I didn't know many years ago that when the Lord speaks it is like apples of gold. You must adhere to the Holy Spirit when He speaks. His words are precious, and He does not waste His words. They are to be taken seriously. The **result** of walking in obedience is the book that you are reading now made manifest for His glory, hallelujah!

He called the children of God the priests, and Kings of the earth, and He is expecting us to walk in our delegated authority to subdue, overcome, overtake, and recover all in the name of Jesus. He called us to live in our wealthy place just like He told the children of Israel. But you must go through the process.

God has an inheritance for His children, but you must contend for every word spoken over your life. The Word of the Lord is precious. Make haste, children of God, go and get what rightfully belongs to you. Your confession of the Word of God should be your profession. You have a legal right to take what belongs to you. As the children of Israel continued to advance throughout the regions and nations, they walked into their promised place, their inheritance. Just as the children of Israel realized, their choices either produced victory or defeat. So likewise, as you read this devotion on choices, you have been given the option to choose life or death, blessing or curses for your life. The Lord is saying, "I am the life-giver. I made this walk easier than man scripted it to be when they added religion to my Word. When you obey my words, you will see the manifestation of my glory in your life. I said this to you, my child, choose life because I am the bread of life."

The God of Israel told Moses that he would lead the children of Israel into the promised land. There would be all the provisions that they needed in that land, and they would have every resource made available to them that was the prophecy. However, whenever a prophecy or word is released over your life, remember that once Satan hears the word, he will begin to contend for it. He will put every obstacle in your way to cause you to abort the promises of God spoken over you. He is not going to lay down and let you walk into your victory without a fight. He is contending for your faith.

Prayer

You have allowed me to choose life or death. I choose life and life more abundantly. I will conquer every valley and desert place in my life by speaking the Word of God. I will submit myself under the mighty hand of God through submission, obedience, and listening to the prophet that you sent to be a blessing to my life. I renounce haughtiness, pride, rebellion, stubbornness, being stiff-necked, and thinking my way is the right way, but it only delays and destruction. I choose walking in the way of righteousness for your name's sake. You have already equipped me to win every battle if I put my trust in you. I am more than a conqueror through Christ who strengthens me. I choose to hear the voice of the good shepherd and a stranger I will not follow. I choose you, Lord, and submit to the Holy Spirit's direction and instruction for my life so that I can continue to go from faith to faith and glory to glory. In Jesus' name. Amen.

Atmospheric Shift

Spiritual warfare is real! The early church in the New Testament dealt with religious manipulators, divination, and various spiritual warfare because of their stance on Jesus. They knew in whom they believed and walked to demonstrate power and authority after the ascension of Jesus Christ. There are times when we can look at someone else's life and say I want to be like this person or that person. You may be looking at the favor on the person's life or ministry or envying their marriage or career and wonder why you are not experiencing that in your life. When you allow the seed of bitterness, grief, doubt, unbelief, strife, rebellion, anger, resentment, jealousy, etc. to take root in your life, you will open demonic portals giving the enemy direct access to your life. As a result, you will experience attacks that may not be warranted or scheduled for you. I can hear some of you saying, "But I have confessed Christ as Savior and Lord of my life. I read the Word of God, but still see barely any breakthrough, no deliverance." You are wondering why these things are happening to you. These things can paralyze your faith and trust me when I say, I get it.

When you become doubtful and weary, the enemy wants to bring you down. Satan is after your faith and focus. He knows if he can bombard you with distractions and cares of the world, you will not fulfill your God-given assignment. He plans to abort your destiny and relationship with God so that you will end up in eternal, everlasting fire with him. So let's keep it real. He is after your soul. The serpent wants to speak lies and deceit in your ear, and if you do not recognize the enemy's voice, it can lead to oppression and depression.

I believe that it is important at this moment that I share when I was experiencing a lot of spiritual warfare. I had been working on a new job assignment for a while and had met a few ladies. We all talked about the Lord so I was automatically assuming that we were all believers until one day conversations came up and to my surprise, we were not all talking about the same God. Or shall I say we all were in different places in our belief systems.

One person was talking about spells and doing all kinds of rituals to keep spirits out of their homes, another person had a Wiccan book which is witchcraft and others were talking about Jesus Christ. I have never been ashamed of the Lord or to proclaim my faith and this situation was no different. Once I began to talk about Jesus, the Messiah, I remember I would experience things out of the ordinary happening in my home. One of the ladies asked me if I had certain things in my home and she told me what the object was and what the color represented. To tell the truth, it was a little unnerving at first until I realized who I was dealing with.

I began to experience demonic warfare in my home. I had to continually pray and read the Word of God to get strategies and downloads from Holy Spirit on how to deal with this level of warfare. It took a while and it was very exhausting, but by the grace of God, I experienced deliverance and breakthrough from that situation. I am here to tell you that spiritual warfare is real people. But this I can say as well, they are not match with the Holy Spirit. He is the atmosphere shifter, and it is always a win, win if you stay the course and let Him lead you. By the way, I can tell you this, I cut those individuals off from my life immediately.

Let us get back to the topic at hand. A spiritual serpent comes to mesmerize you, fill your life with fear, dread, disappointment, and poverty constricting you so that you cannot move forward, which causes you to shrink in the spirit. This spirit comes to shut your mouth and paralyze you with fear. The python spirit causes you to feel heavy with excessive burdens and attacks you mentally, spiritually, physically, emotionally, and financially. This spirit comes to overwhelm you and torment your soul, leaving you frustrated, doubting God, when it looks as if you see no advancement in your life, and some have even quit God. The spiritual serpent is a beguiling spirit that controls you and targets the soul, which is your mind, will, and emotions.

In the natural, when a serpent targets an individual, it moves methodically to attack its next victim. The snake, specifically the python, hisses in the victim's ear, which is a distraction as it begins to coil around the victim and tightens its grip to immobilize the person. It continues to tighten the grip, breaking the bones as it crushes the victim. Its mouth enlarges as it swallows the victim whole. The python can go many months without eating because certain large prey can slow down its metabolism. In like manner, when Satan is devouring you, he digests you slowly, causing one disruption to your life after another. He will consume you if you do not discern him and take authority by fighting the good fight of faith.

The spiritual serpent speaks lies in your ear, and if you do not focus on the voice of God when it speaks, you will receive the serpent's bites.

A person should take ownership of the thoughts that they hear in their conscious mind. When you hear something in your mind that is harmful, negative and does not agree with your thought processes, do not dismiss it and assume that the thought came from you. Instead, you should immediately cast down the idea or reject it, so it does not take root and become a stronghold in your mind. When you have allowed this to go on for some time, maybe even years, one will develop strongholds that are now controlling your life, leading to self-sabotage, defeat, anguish, disappointment, and if severe enough, maybe even death.

The serpent spirit swallows your dreams, aspirations, goals, your purpose, and desires. Your desires include the desire to live because of all the poison of the serpent's conversations that went unchecked. When a person is overwhelmed by defeat and a lack of movement forward, they can misdiagnose the situation and feel deserted and abandoned by God. They may not detect spiritual warfare because they are not in tune with the correct frequency in the spirit realm. By this I mean, that when a person is in tune with the Holy Spirit as a believer you can identify the voice of the Lord because you know His characteristics regardless of the method, He choices to speak. You are familiar with His voice. This takes practice so that you will be able to distinguish your thoughts from the Holy Spirit's thoughts, words, and instructions. They are operating from the soul realm and not the spirit realm, where they can pick up the frequency of heaven through prayer, praise, meditation, supplication, and thanksgiving. The Websters 1828 Dictionary defines the soul as the spiritual, rational, and immortal substance in man, which distinguishes him from brutes; that part of man which enables him to think and reason, and which renders him a subject of moral government. The soul is your mind, will, and emotions. The spirit came from God the Father which is in supernatural form housed in your body.

When the serpent attacks, it zaps your spiritual strength. It becomes hard to hear from God. You are offended because you may be praying and do not see a change in your circumstances. You may be living from check to check, with no stability in life or peace because of the intense warfare over extended periods. The poison of the serpent's communication injected lies in your soul and has you in a tailwind of confusion. Nothing makes sense in your life. The enemy wants to keep you confused, tormented in your mind, and walking in condemnation. Therefore, you must respond to the enemy from a spiritual perspective by speaking the Word of God.

Psalm 91:13 (NLT)

You will trample upon lions and cobras; you will crush fierce lions and serpents under your feet.

Another characteristic of the python spirit is that you may become so emotionally driven that you blame God for what is going on. You believe He does not love you and ignores you. Although you are saved, tithing, going to church, helping others, and working in ministry, you see limited breakthroughs and blessings. You may have sought deliverance but did not receive it and are now upset and angry because you have discerned enough to know that something is not right, but you cannot figure out what is happening in your life. You have been able to identify that this is not normal and that whatever it is, God can deliver you from it, but it has not happened yet. You know that you are serving an almighty God that can deliver you but has chosen not at that moment which causes despair and hopelessness. So you begin to withdraw from God and spiritually decline in your faith. Because you may be saying, how many times can I pray, fast, seek deliverance, attend church, read the Word of God, and be looked at by others as if something is wrong with me? There is a natural and spiritual stagnation going on, and you see little to no fruit manifestations in your life.

Hold on, I say to you, hold on! God is not through with you yet. Do not allow this spirit to cause you to feel like an orphan, causing you to want to be left alone because you may feel rejected by God and people. You may have the desire to distance yourself from people and not understand why. The enemy wants to isolate you so he can continue to inject his lies and venom into your mind, will, and emotions while you are weak in faith.

There are other ways that the serpent attacks, such as in your subconscious mind using people, dreams, experiences, and life in general. Therefore, it is up to you what you allow in your ear gates, eye gates, to go into your soul, come out of your mouth, and seed in your heart. According to Matthew 15:11 (AMP), "it is not what goes into the mouth of a man that defiles and dishonors him, but what comes out of the mouth, this defile and dishonors him."

Pause, take a moment, and think about what is happening every time you start to feel overwhelmed, unloved, and undervalued in life. Exhale at this moment and breathe. Take the time to collect your thoughts and not allow your thoughts and emotions to dictate to you. Remember, you are in control. It is your life; therefore, choose life! Speak Life and not death over your situation. Even when you cannot track or trace God, and He feels so far away from you, or you feel abandoned, you owe it to yourself to muster up enough strength to say that God loves me, and I trust Him. If you are someone that experiences one setback after the next, without relief, know that you are someone that is a threat to the Kingdom of darkness. The enemy does not put a lot of effort into people that already belong to him. Therefore, you must shift your focus on Jesus and not the trial or testing you are in so that the sword does not devour you.

Let us look at what the Word of God says according to John 10:10 (AMP) "The thief comes only to steal and kill and destroy. I came that they may have and enjoy life, and have it in abundance [to the full, till it overflows.]" That is a praise break moment right there! So come on, no matter how you are feeling, stop, put this book down, and give God praise. He loved you enough to find this chapter in the book to lead you to a new way of thinking and self-deliverance from the python spirit. So now, trust and believe; you must roll up your sleeves and fight the good fight of faith because your life and destiny are on the line.

You may have been crying, feeling sorry for yourself, and stuck in a pity party about the injustice of it all, but guess what? If you are a believer, you have the Holy Spirit living on the inside of you, and I command in the name of Jesus that you arise, take up your bed and walk. You will no longer be the victim of the serpent's bite. You are victorious in Jesus Christ. Hallelujah! Lord, we give you all the praise, glory, and honor, and trust you to believe that you will not leave anyone in the den of lions and serpents.

Romans 8:37 (AMP)

Yet in all these things we are more than conquerors and gain an overwhelming victory through Him who loved us [so much that He died for us.

The more you stay in God using your spiritual weapons of praise, worship, reading the Word of God, and creating an atmosphere in your home, and at work that is conducive for the glory to show up, the fewer attacks you will have. Praise God until you receive complete deliverance from the hands of the enemy. As you stay consistent in your communion with the Lord and allow Holy Spirit to give you strategies to defeat and overcome the enemy, your spirit man will become stronger and stronger. You will no longer just read the Word of God as a ritual but will take on the stance of a soldier in the army of the Lord that knows how to command their morning, day, and night. As a believer in Jesus Christ, you have authority, rule, and dominion to operate as a god on earth. The spiritual oil you receive because God's Word has become your necessary food in the spirit builds spiritual muscle in your spirit man.

At all costs, one must stay in a posture to hear Holy Spirit when He speaks and obey His instructions. I can hear you now saying, but it is not as easy as you are saying or making it out to be, Yes, that is correct. I am not saying that it will be easy. If you look at the disciples in the New Testament, they went through trials of being mocked, beaten, stoned, persecuted, and even beaten to death, but they stood for Jesus. Why did the disciples endure so much pain and forsook all for the gospel's sake? Their eyes were set on the reward of the eternal life that is to come?

Romans 8:18 (AMP) says, "For I consider [from the standpoint of faith] that the sufferings of the present life are not worthy to be compared with the glory that is about to be revealed to us and in us!" I am here to tell you that you need the anointing of God in your life. The anointing comes from your trials and tests. You must pass these tests, which increases your capacity in God each time you win. You cannot quit; forge on like a good soldier.

Someone reading this right now can identify with what I am saying, but you are tired. It has been a long time in this battle, and you feel defeated because it feels like there is no end in sight. Now that you have made that statement let me pose this question to you. Where would you have been in the difficult place had God not been there with you? Be honest before you start forming an emotional opinion or statement in your defense. I can surely tell you that you will not be able to make it without the grace of God in your life. The enemy wants you to quit, thus aborting your God-given purpose, walking away from God altogether, which will lead to your spiritual and natural death in its due season. You will not be able to survive without the oil (anointing) and Jesus. Therefore, you must not reduce yourself to a casual Christian who will become a causality of war.

In the natural, they say there is a snake line. There is an atmosphere in the mountains where snakes can only go up so high up, and once they cross this invisible line, they will die because of the altitude. Think about that. They have limitations and are restricted based on atmospheric changes. In the spirit realm, when dealing with this serpent spirit, you can only be defeated when you live from a low altitude in the spirit.

When someone is not praying, reading the Word, worshipping, not taking authority over the situation, but listening to the serpent whispering in their ear, it is wreaking havoc in their life because of the low altitude they are positioned at as a believer. Once they take ownership of what is going on and decide they no longer want to be victims, they will take out their spiritual weapons and fight for their salvation and legal right to rule.

Ephesians 6:10-17 (AMP)

be strong in the Lord [draw your strength from Him and be empowered through your union with Him] and in the power of His [boundless] might. Put on the full armor of God [for His precepts are like the splendid armor of a heavily-armed soldier], so that you may be able to [successfully] stand up against all the schemes and the strategies and the deceits of the devil. For our struggle is not against flesh and blood [contending only with physical opponents], but against the rulers, against the powers, against the world forces of this [present] darkness, against the spiritual forces of wickedness in the heavenly (supernatural) places. Therefore, put on the complete armor of God, so that you will be able to [successfully] resist and stand your ground in the evil day [of danger], and having done everything [that the crisis demands], to stand firm [in your place, fully prepared, immovable, victorious]. So stand firm and hold your ground, having [a]tightened the wide band of truth (personal integrity, moral courage) around your waist and having put on the breastplate of righteousness (an upright heart), and having strapped on your feet the gospel of peace in preparation [to face the enemy with firm-footed stability and the readiness produced by the good news]. Above all, lift up the [protective] shield of faith with which you can extinguish all the flaming arrows of the evil one. And take the helmet of salvation, and the sword of the Spirit, which is the Word of God.

So, what are you waiting for, child of God? Fight! 1 John 5:4 (AMP), says, "For everyone born of God is victorious and overcomes the world; and this is the victory that has conquered and overcome the world—our [continuing, persistent] faith [in Jesus the Son of God]." The enemy is contending for your faith. He contends for your God-ordained purpose, and he is attempting to silence your voice if you stand for Jesus Christ.

The Lord may be allowing the attacks, these life-altering changes in your life, but He is not trying to take something from you. Jesus is trying to get something to you. The Lord knows that if certain things don't happen, the potential He spoke into you before the foundations of the world will not manifest. There will be disruptions to your life that will draw you closer to Jesus when you don't obey the prompting of the Holy Spirit. It will not always feel good, but we walk by faith, not by sight, and we walk with assurance in Jesus, who is walking with us through every step of the difficult situations we face in life.

Jesus loves us and has invested too much time into us for us to shrink back and coward down to the enemy.

Luke 10:19 (NIV)

I have given you authority to trample on snakes and scorpions and to overcome all the power of the enemy; nothing will harm you.

In the spirit, we can live in victory above the invisible snake line. We must use our spiritual weapons of praise, thanksgiving, praying the scriptures through declarations and prayer, reading the Word of God, fasting, worshipping, praying in the spirit, and sitting before the Lord in solitude to hear your next instructions. We must live well-pleasing lives to God, which is our reasonable service unto Him in humility. If you accepted Jesus Christ as your Lord and Savior, a part of that condition is that you have chosen to die to yourself daily and to live by the Holy Spirit leading and guiding your life. You represent the King of Glory on the earth, so daughters of Zion and men of Valor arise and shine, take your position, walk in your authority, dominion, and rule. Regardless of what the enemy throws at you, you are an atmosphere shifter who is sitting in silence waiting for the instructions of the commander to give you the necessary downloads to achieve your victory in Jesus name.

Prayer

Lord, I want to say thank you for being merciful to me in my difficult times. I may not always understand what is happening, but I know that you protect me from the enemy. In the name of Jesus, I bind the python spirit that causes fatigue, frustration, weariness, oppression, depression, fear, and anxiety. I command every tormenting spirit in my mind, will, and emotions to come out of me in the name of Jesus. I bind every strongman in my life and break your power and command you to leave me now in Jesus' name.

Lord, I repent for opening satanic doors through doubt, unbelief, murmuring, and complaining. I break all soul ties with these spirits, all spirit groupings working against me, and all ruling spirits operating against my life in Jesus' name. I break, destroy, and separate myself from all covenants, contracts, and agreements, knowing and unknowing that I have made with Satan that have caused me to be attacked by these spirits. I renounced them now in the name of Jesus, and I command them to go to the abyss, to dry places in Jesus' name, never to return to my family or me. I receive life and life more abundantly in every area of my life. In Jesus' name, I pray. Amen.

Glory Carrier

We are living in a day and time where things are instantaneous. Some want everything at their fingertips in a moment. Technology continues to advance and evolve like never before. They are making robots that look more like humans that can process and hold more data than humans. If we are not careful, we must consider the possibility that too much technology will replace our jobs and human interaction. The creator of the universe did not create us to be a substitute or to become secondary to technology. He created us in His image and likeness to rule, reign, and be His ambassadors on the earth. He does not need technology to be the object that injects things into the minds of His creation.

We must be careful not to allow external forces to be the sole object of our desires. I am not saying that technology or other influences are the total blame because we make a conscious decision that determines our outcome. Think about it for a moment. If you are watching television, on the phone, or on social media for hours, how much time is left for Holy Spirit? How many hours have you penciled in to spend with Holy Spirit? You will feed your spirit man and soul the world's things if you listen to secular things more than spiritual ones. If you are not feeding your spirit spiritual food, what do you believe will be the outcome of that?

Let us bring this aspect into the equation. You can also consume your time with spiritual things, reading the Word, praying, fasting, and worshipping, but still find that you are missing it with God. By that, I mean we can do all the spiritual calisthenics and still be missing it with the Lord if there is no balance by incorporating Holy Spirit.

After He ascended to heaven, Jesus charged the disciples to be His representatives on earth and walk in His glorious power and authority. Jesus said when the comforter comes; He will show you things to come. Therefore, the disciples had the promise of Holy Spirit with them to lead and guide them. First, they watched Jesus perform notable signs, wonders, and miracles. Then, He commissioned them to do the same after His ascension.

The disciples grew and developed intimate encounters with the Lord while He was on earth. They knew their teacher had left them to fulfill the great commission to go out into all the world and proclaim the gospel, the good news of Jesus. What do you think it would take for the disciples to walk in the authority and power that Jesus walked in while He was here on earth? Jesus had an avid prayer life. He was disciplined and was the wellsprings of life. He was the giver of life, loved unparalleled, didn't complain, walked in humility like no other, forgave his enemies without hesitation, was forever merciful, full of wisdom, and had thought-provoking wit that angered His enemies.

Jesus was cool and very relatable. He did not look like what the Pharisees expected. He was not adorned in a purple or scarlet robe with a crown on his head and jewelry dripping off; he came to serve, not to be served. He exuded the ultimate level of grace and humility while walking in complete confidence, wisdom, knowledge, counsel, might, understanding, and righteousness. He would get up a great while before day and pray to His heavenly Father. Why do you think He would get up early before the beginning of the day? Jesus knows that the adversary is always plotting and planning an attack against the people of God. He knew that it was imperative to get instructions from His Heavenly Father on where He should go, what town, city, and location. He knew who He would contact because God scheduled people for a date with destiny and the King.

Jesus was on assignment not of Himself but on the assignment of God to save, heal, teach the disciples about the kingdom, and deliver His people out of the bondage of the enemy. Jesus came to set the captives free. We must remember that Jesus did not come to the earth as God. He came in the form of man and conquered every attempt of Satan to sabotage His assignment in the flesh. Hallelujah! Hold up, wait a minute. Let's put praise on that statement. Jesus did not come to the earth as God. He would have been illegal because He had given the earth to man. Therefore, He had to come as a man to defeat sin as fully man without sin.

I know this statement may sound farfetched but let us go there. If Jesus came to the earth as a man and defeated sin in the flesh, do you think we can't do so as well? It is something to think about. We miss the mark and sin at times because we are not crucifying our flesh. We fall victim to temptations, the desires of the flesh, and Satan's subtle coercions and tactics.

Let's shift gears here. I know you think I forgot about the glory. Absolutely not! That was a prerequisite to segue into conversations about the glory. I desire to make statements that will provoke you to journey deeper in God. The level you go in God depends strictly on you.

One day, when I was young in the Lord, I told Him that I wanted more of Him. I wanted these supernatural encounters with Him. I heard to Lord say to me, "How bad do you want it? Will you discipline yourself and do whatever I ask of you? Will you sacrifice your life for me? Will you say yes to my will? Will you forsake all for me? Did you count the cost of salvation, my daughter? It will cost you everything?" I'll tell you the truth. I had no idea what the Lord was saying to me because I was only maybe two or three years in the Lord and did not understand a lot of things scripturally.

I knew that the level of intimacy I desired to walk in, signs, wonders, and miracles would require my total surrender to the Lord. I wanted to walk in the anointing that the prophets from the Old Testament and Smith Wigglesworth. Smith Wigglesworth was from England. He was a Pentecostal preacher who had unwavering faith and a love for God. This minister of the gospel lived a very surrendered life to the Holy Spirit. He by the grace of God performed many notable miracles, healing, and deliverance in the lives of the people. He had unwavering faith and at times did unorthodox things that he said the Holy Spirit say to do and people would be healed. One example was punching someone in the stomach, however, the person was healed or delivered. He also raised the dead by the power of the Holy Spirit. You can look at someone's life and see the polished version where they have been processed and are walking tall in the anointing, but you have no idea what it took for them to get there. I learned this valuable lesson; don't ask vicariously for things you do not know the repercussions of.

When one decides to walk in this realm, it is not free. It can cost you your life and sacrifice yourself to the Lord in total surrender.

2 Corinthians 4:17 (NIV)

For our light and momentary troubles are achieving for us an eternal glory that far outweighs them all.

To tap into the glory, let me correct that statement; you don't want to just tap into the glory. You want to live in this realm of God where the unforeseeable is at your disposal. The unseen realm is made available to you only by the permission of the King. You walk as a god in this place, as you were intended to walk from the beginning. In this realm, you have face-to-face encounters with the Lord. He will pull back the veil and give you exclusive access to Him because you have disciplined yourself. He has found you worthy to enter in and said, "access granted." He wants to know, "Will you carry my glory? Will you say no to what is trendy in society today? Will you follow the road less traveled? Will you put the food down and pick up my Word? Will you sit before me in my presence for hours if need be? Do you want to have an insatiable desire to sit with me and learn? Do you want to hear what the Spirit wants to say to you? Will you get upset if you sit for hours and hear nothing? How can two walk together except they agree? Will you stop trying to win me over to your way of thinking and learn to submit to my will for your life?

This is another Selah moment. Be honest with yourself. These are reflection moments. Put the book down, go back to the questions, and have those honest conversations with the Lord. He is waiting on you. When you are ready, let's continue.

What does a Glory Carrier do? They can heal the sick, raise the dead, open blinded eyes, move into the spirit realm, and understand the mystery of God as the Holy Spirit gives them. You will not walk as a mere man or woman. You have supernatural abilities because you are a spirit that lives in a body. We can walk on water also, not only in the spirit realm. Those encounters were not only limited to those in the Bible, but we must believe with unwavering faith.

The Lord wants His children to know so much more about Him, but you must walk pure and holy circumspectly before Him as a lifestyle in these realms. This is available to us if we seek, obey, trust, follow and desire not the things, but the giver of the things. Psalm 84:11 (NLT) says, "For the Lord God is our sun and our shield. He gives us grace and glory. The Lord will withhold no good thing from those who do what is right." If God's glory is limited to the people of the Old Testament, that will make the Lord partial. He said in His word that He is not a respecter of people. God respects his principles. So, I ask you this question, how bad do you want the anointing?

I am not speaking of a person tapping into the spirit realm illegally by practicing divination, seeking psychics, and astral projections. These are real methods to move into the spirit realm, but you are entering in via satanic occultic powers from Satan. That is dangerous. If you have ever gone through these channels to tap into the spirit realm, please stop now and ask the Lord to forgive you for using sorcery that is not of the Lord. There are dire consequences for engaging with Satan in this manner. I am speaking of a relationship with Holy Spirit the safe way, by his leading. This is not about having out-of-body experiences. Seeking the Lord and walking in the glory is about you being open to the Lord, what He may desire to do through you, with you, for you, and to you.

Who is the point of reference for Glory? Holy Spirit! Let's break out of tradition. Have no agenda other than to please Holy Spirit. Love on Him and give Him your undivided attention. He is not some abstract being. He is a person, the spirit of God, who is alive and well. Lose your inhibitions and die to yourself. Let your hair down, and come to Him just the way you are. Share your most intimate desires with Him. Obtaining the glory starts with intimacy and honesty. Pray to God to give you the heart to love the things that He loves and hate the things that He hates. You will begin to tap into the heart of God. Ask Him to cleanse you of all impurities and everything that is not like Him.

You will begin to take on the characteristics of God. Ask the Lord to hide you so that only He is seen in you. As you start to yield and obey His instructions, you are becoming one with Him. The more you seek His face and not His hand, you will begin to tap into the glory realm.

2 Thessalonians 3:5 (NLT)

In the glory realm you will soar like an eagle.

Colossians 3:12 (NIV)

Therefore, as God's chosen people, holy and dearly loved, clothe yourselves with compassion, kindness, humility, gentleness, and patience.

When you are in the glory realm, you are not living according to the dictates of the flesh. It is spirit to spirit. Your thoughts have changed, your posture has changed, and there is no desire to live below your creation. In the glory realm, your daily interactions with Holy Spirit will lead you to be more sensitive to Him as you become one with the Word.

As a Glory Carrier, you are weighty in the spirit. You walk tall in the anointing because your life has exemplified discipline and trusting in Holy Spirit. You have crucified your flesh because you understand that Jesus was not only in the Bible, but He is real to you, literally jumping off the pages for you. You walk in such a place in the Lord that someone can't distinguish you from King Jesus. You will experience, move, and live in the realm with the supernatural power and prevail against the enemy. Matthew 5:8 (KJV) says, "Blessed are the pure in heart: for they shall see God."

I remember an encounter that I had when I was praying as a baby believer. I was in my room and was in the presence of God for a while. Suddenly, I felt the atmosphere shift, and I sensed something was about to happen. I began to feel uneasy and was unsure of what was about to happen. Then I felt a thick presence come into my bedroom, and suddenly it moved to the side of my bed near the window. It began to take shape, and I could see a part of an angel's wing. The wing was the whitest white I had very seen. I could see the scalloped wings in detail, and there was a presence of light around the wing, which was the glory. Then, I did the unthinkable. Although I knew it was an angel, I became fearful and walked out of the room.

It hurts me to think about that because I missed out on an encounter with my angel. Just as quickly as the presence was forming, it left because of my fear. So, child of God, don't ask for deeper, then when the opportunity arises, allow fear to grip you and cause you to miss the encounter.

If you have had a spiritual encounter and reacted the same way, do not beat yourself up about it. The Lord knows your reactions before they happen. It's not for Him; it's for you to see where you are. Don't allow this to stop you from seeking the greater things in God. Remember He knows your heart. He knows what you can handle, and he has a million ways to reveal Himself to you. So please stay open and allow Him to show Himself to you in the way that He chooses.

If you are ready to go to another level in God, say, "Lord, I want more. I want to go higher. I want to be in sync with you. Holy Spirit teach me the rhythm of God. I want to flow in the Spirit. I want to be one with you. Lord, I desire to be one with you like Jesus is one with the Father."

When He sees that you are serious and you realize this is not a microwave gesture or a momentary feeling but a lifelong commitment, put Him to the test. Become a God Chaser! If you stay faithful in your pursuit of Him, He will say, "Wait a minute, who is this that is so persistent to seek me out in their secret place at all costs? Who is this that knows how to touch my heart and flow in my rhythm and heartbeat? Who is this that desires me over everything and everyone else and is in hot pursuit of me?" In your persistent pursuit of Him, don't be surprised if the tables turn and He begins to pursue you.

Someone may be reading this chapter thinking it is impossible to have that kind of relationship with the Lord. I say to you, "If you only believe, all things are possible."

If the Old Testament prophets could do it with their flaws without the Holy Spirit living inside of them, so can you because you have the added advantage of the Spirit living inside you. The question is, do you desire that level of intimacy? If you do not want that level of commitment or intimacy that produces the glory, it doesn't make you any less loved by the Father. He loves you regardless. I asked the question to let you know that this level of power through intimacy, consecration, dedication, obedience to His instructions is available for you if you want it.

If you desire to be a Glory Carrier, ask yourself what is stopping you? Do you think that He is worth the sacrifice? You may not want to pay the price to get this level of anointing, which is also ok. It doesn't make you less if that is not your desire. These questions are not judgment zone. I want you to have a conversation with Holy Spirit to help you go to another level. Don't be comfortable with where you are; there is always more in Jesus.

The point of this chapter is do not limit the Lord. You should always desire to go higher, and that could look different for each of us. All that I am saying is don't settle for less or average when you have Holy Spirit inside of you. Ask Holy Spirit to expand your capacity to new levels of thinking and a deeper intimacy to duplicate Jesus on the earth with demonstrations of signs, wonders, and miracles. Ask Him to give you the mind of Christ. You have not because you ask not. Soar Eagle Soar!

Prayer

Heavenly Father, I simply ask you to take me higher. I want to know you more deeply. Please help me, Holy Spirit, to take the limits off. In Jesus' name. Amen.

A Date with the King

How often have you eliminated the distractions, turned off all social media and television, stopped allowing these platforms to tell you about their vision for your life, and sat quietly before the Lord, waiting to hear Holy Spirit speak to you? Were you antsy when you did not hear a word after ten, twenty, thirty minutes, or more, and you decided that I guess He does not want to say anything to me today? So, you jumped up and went about your daily activities. Have you considered a date with the Holy Spirit? If you are single, have you ever set a place at the table for the Lord so that the Lord can eat with you. When I say the Lord wants to eat with you, I mean He wants to impart His wisdom to you. You can make the time memorable by taking out your best china and saying, "Lord, I want to invite you into my day. It's just you and I." Do you know how significant that is to the Lord? Do you know how many people do not acknowledge Him at all on any given day?

Start your morning by saying, "Good morning Holy Spirit. I welcome you into my day to lead and guide me. Holy Spirit, what do you want to do today? Holy Spirit, what is on your heart today? I want to please you, therefore whatever you say goes. I don't have an agenda for this day. I have blocked off this time for me to listen to your instructions. I am open and available to you because I honor you and treasure the words that drop off your lips like apples of gold."

Plan a date with the risen King by carving out an allotted amount of time out of your busy day to talk to Him. But please do not be structured with time you block off for the Lord and do not watch the clock as if you are restricting time spent with Him. You must be pliable and shift when the Lord moves because He is not on your schedule. He must be reverenced and held in the highest esteem and not reduced to your selfish desires. No, this time is exclusively for Jesus. Ask Him what He likes, how was His day, and what you can do for Him today? Have genuine heartfelt conversations with the Lord.

We look at Him as this great God of the universe, and He is. However, He is still a person who has emotions, a soul, hurts when we hurt, cries, and carries the world's burdens on His shoulders. He is not on vacation in heaven. He is working with the assistance of His angels to protect and provide for you. He is listening and responding to the concerns of people all over the world at once. It could be possible that He is not answering the questions in the way we always want Him to, but He answers them according to the grace on your life. Considering all these things that we may take for granted, do you not see that the Father wants to hear from His children? If He created you, don't you think that He wants fellowship with you.

Make every effort to carve out time for the Lord. Be sure to have paper, pencil, a recorder, or whatever method you choose to capture the moments as He speaks to you.

Let me interject here for a moment. If you are distracted with carnal thoughts while sitting in the presence of the Lord, quickly cast them down so that they are not overpowering and clouding your thought processes, so you don't miss what He says.

Jeremiah 24:7 (NET)

I will give them the desire to acknowledge that I am the Lord. I will be their God and they will be my people. For they will wholeheartedly return to me.

If it takes you listening to worship music, instrumental whatever quiets your soul so that you can make the appropriate connection in the spirit realm. You need to become one with Holy Spirit. You must empty yourself so that He can pour into you. You must become one with Holy Spirit, spirit to Spirit.

As I stated at the beginning of this conversation, if you don't hear from Him in thirty minutes or less, don't be inconsiderate and jump up like He is not worth you waiting. Even if He says nothing in the time that you have allotted for Him, be patient and respectful of your quiet time in His presence. How are you handling Holy Spirit? Please sit in expectation with eager anticipation to hear from the King of Glory.

Psalm 46:10 (NKJV)

Be still and know that I am God; I will be exalted among the nations, I will be exalted in the earth!

When we are on a natural date, we get dressed in a favorite attire because we want to please ourselves and our partners. We want to look good and smell good. In other words, we want to make a good impression on our date. How much more of a good impression should we make on our date with Holy Spirit? Holy Spirit wants you to love on Him. Converse with Him, sing to Him, and stroke His ego. He deserves that. If you can put on your best attire for your earthly partner, why can't you do that for your spiritual partner, the paraclete?

I will share a transparent moment with you. I have set aside time for Holy Spirit, and when I did not hear from Him over a certain amount of time, I would jump up and start worshipping Him. I have even left His presence and started doing other things that had nothing to do with spending time with Him. I remember times I said I was going to get in the presence of the Lord, but I didn't focus on Him. The worship music would be playing, but I was distracted. I would start worshipping, but thoughts of food or a chore that I needed to take care of would dominate my thoughts, and I would become agitated. Because of the distractive thoughts, one of two things would happen. I would give in to the thoughts of food or start doing the chores, etc. Or the worship music played, and I would stop and take authority over the enemy. For the record, most always, I would assume authority over the thoughts by bringing them into subjection to the word of God.

Your soul has a voice, and it speaks loud when you do not have the discipline to tell it what to do. Instead, you choose to yield to its voice. On the flip side, there are times when I am in the presence of the Lord, and I will dance before Him. In my mind, I will visualize having my hands extended toward Him as if

He is taking my hands and twirling me around. I laugh in the presence of the Lord. I then imagine that I am twirling Him around, and He must duck down to circle in my arms because He is taller than I am. I envision that He and I are performing the waltz dance. Those are precious moments for me because I lose myself in Him. I don't allow my mind to say, what are you doing? In those moments, I realize anything that may have weighed me down in the day's events has fallen off me in His presence, and I am left feeling light as a feather. That is what being in His presence does. When you can rest in His arms, you have completely given Him your cares and yokes and have submitted to Holy Spirit, and you have taken on the yokes of the Lord. It is then and only then that you can truly exhale and as they say, let go and let God!

Holy Spirit knows what we need, and He wants to refresh you in His presence. He wants to reset your day in His presence without you giving Him a laundry list of things you want Him to do for you. Instead, He wants to strengthen your spirit, pour into you, love on you, spirit to spirit, and heart to heart. Will you invite Him to join you? Will you allow Holy Spirit to sit upon the throne of your heart? Will you have a date with the King? Will you not just pencil Him in so that you can say that you filled your quota for the day? Instead, take this moment to take inventory of your devotional time and see what the areas of weakness are, and ask Holy Spirit to strengthen you in these areas so that your communing time with the Lord will be the most effective.

I challenge you to invite Holy Spirit to pull up to the table with you and dine with you. It would behoove you to feast in the presence of the Lord. The Lord says, "Please come eat and drink at my table." The Lord will give you fresh oil in His presence. Please make room for the Spirit of God to sup with you.

Estella Smith

Psalm 23:5-6, (AMP)

You prepare a table before me in the presence of my enemies. You have anointed and refreshed my head with oil; My cup overflows. Surely goodness and mercy and unfailing love shall follow me all the days of my life, And I shall dwell forever [throughout all my days] in the house and in the presence of the Lord.

My mind goes to the wedding supper with the Lamb. Oh, what a marvelous time that will be at the marriage supper with the Lamb. We can practice His presence here on earth as a prelude to what is coming.

He has a table of blessings waiting for us in His presence. The Word of God says in Psalms 16:11 (AMP), "You will show me the path of life; In Your presence is fullness of joy in Your right hand there are pleasures forevermore." Hallelujah!

Prayer

Heavenly Father, I will empty myself so that you can fill me with your wisdom. I want to give you my heart, not my hand of inhibitions. I want to sit at the table with the King of Glory and allow you to wash me clean and purify me in your presence. I want to eat the bread of life and drink from the river of life with the Holy Spirit. You have set the table before me, and you are asking me to come into your presence Lord, and I accept. I bless your holy name. In Jesus' name, I pray. Amen.

Seed, Time, Harvest

Have you taken the time to assess your life fully? At least once a year, you may go to the doctor to get a yearly exam because you want to make sure that you are healthy, and if you do have a concern, the doctor can diagnose you at your appointment. You talk to the doctor and share your medical history and physical health since your last doctor's visit. The Lord wants to care for our emotional, physical, spiritual, financial, and relational needs as well. Let me pose this question to you. Have you considered a spiritual physical? The Word of God says, 3 John 1:2 (TPT), "Beloved friend, I pray that you are prospering in every way and that you continually enjoy good health, just as your soul is prospering." When you look at this verse, it indicates that the Lord is not only interested in your physical health but your soul, which is your mind, will, and emotions.

The Lord desires that we are whole in every area of our lives. There are times when we may not understand what the Lord may be doing in our lives, but it is in those times that we need to unplug from our regular duties and get in the presence of the Lord. There are things that you may be petitioning the Lord for, and it has been an exceptionally long time, and you have not received an answer to your question. You have assessed the answer is no, instead of seeking the heart of the Lord on the matter.

Abraham is called the Father of faith in the Word of God. God told Abraham that He would make him the Father of many nations.

Romans 4:20-21 (NKJV)

He did not waver at the promise of God through unbelief, but was strengthened in faith, giving glory to God, and being fully convinced that what He had promised He was also able to perform.

What did Abraham have? He had a promise and Word from the Lord. So what did Abraham need to do? First, he needed to water the Word that he heard.

The Word is the seed, your faith, and your confessions water the seed. How do you water the Word? When you stand on the promises of God without wavering concerning the Word that you heard from the Lord, faith begins to arise in you. When you have faith in God, it breeds expectation, expectation breeds hope, and hope brings the manifestation of the promise of God. The Word of God says in Romans 5:5 (NIV) and hope does not put us to shame, because God's love has been poured out into our hearts through the Holy Spirit, who has been given to us. God wants to reveal to you His faithfulness, power, grace, and goodness. It is all in His timing. Do not allow the enemy to rob you of the Lord's promises because you are too antsy and feel as though you can't wait on the Lord. The enemy wants to take your testimony of the goodness of the Lord. Please do not fall victim to Satan's devices.

When you are in the will of God for your life, you will have a steady stream and flow of the favor of God. The goodness and blessings of God will be apparent. You will begin to see that there is a spirit of ease. All provisions are available when you are in the correct place and posture for your assignment.

No, we are not limiting God to needs because that's too low for Him. He wants to take care of you, your wants, and your desires and treat you like royalty. Remember, He is the person that put the desires in you in the first place.

But you may be wondering, how do I know when the Spirit is speaking to me? One example is when you hear something drop in your spirit out of nowhere. You may dismiss it and continue with what you were doing, but you will hear the Word, phrase, or whatever said again. Holy Spirit is trying to get your attention. You will hear it off and on until you realize it's Him. That is the seed He dropped into your spirit. What you do with that seed is entirely up to you.

If the Lord does you like He does with me, I can be doing something nonspiritual, and out of nowhere, I will hear something in my spirit. It is a repeated thought that does not go away. Now, do not get religious on me. I know that every idea is not Holy Spirit. It is pivotal that you discern the voice that you heard and try the spirit by the spirit.

I want to speak a few things over you right now to feed your faith and starve your doubts in Jesus' name. If you have dormant seeds that have not manifested in your life, Father, in the name of Jesus, I ask you to allow the winds of the spirit to blow profusely on the person reading this devotional right now. Lord, resurrect every dormant seed spoken to or over them in the name of Jesus. Holy Spirit brood over them, hoover over them, make every crooked place straight and every rough place smooth in Jesus' name. Release your fire to burn up every stagnant place in their soul Lord so that they don't get tired of watering their seed. I decree that you have the finishers anointing to hear the Word of the Lord for your life. Stand in faith and give glory to God, waiting on the timing of the Lord to manifest your promise. Breathe the breath of life into them, Holy Spirit, and renew your right spirit within them in Jesus' name.

Lord, you desire that we shall have life and life more abundantly. We shall stand in faith like Abraham, giving glory to God, without wavering because you are a man that you do not lie and watch over your Word to perform it in Jesus' name.

I hear the Lord saying, "Dust off the weariness, my child. The vision that I have for you is far-reaching. I have a table spread before you with all the delicacies, treasures, and hidden riches in secret places. Will you come, seek out the desires that I have for you? I am ready to blow your mind. It starts in seed form, which means you must search it out. Does not my Word say, Proverbs 25:2 (AMP) 'It is the glory of God to conceal a matter, But the glory of kings is to search out a matter."

We have been called to dominate, rule, and walk in our dominion. If you have promises that have not manifested in your life yet, what are you waiting for? Speak the Word of God, commune with Holy Spirit, and see the salvation of the Lord in every area of your life in Jesus' name.

Prayer

Father, in all things I give you praise for you are worthy to be honored, glorified, and praised. I thank you that your Word is necessary food for my soul. I will engage you more in intimacy because I desire to draw closer to you. I will take the time to enjoy the journey with you when things seem difficult and not as I have expected. It is in you that I move, live, and have my being. I will stand on the promises of God because the Word is the heartbeat of my soul. When I hear your still small voice speaking to my heart, I will guard and steward that Word with all diligence and will cultivate that Word by praise and thanksgiving. Holy Spirit, help me ponder on the Word of God and get it into my spirit so that it will become life to me and I will be able to speak it like rivers of living waters that quenches my thirsty soul. Holy Spirit, help me to declare your Word without doubt and unbelief so that I will see the manifestation of the goodness of God in every area of my life. In Jesus' name. Amen.

Thank you

I want to take this moment to thank you for reading this worship experience. My prayer is that you participated in the experience in every chapter. The goal is to bring you into a closer walk with Christ Jesus and to bring inner healing to your souls. I want you to always remember no matter what you are facing, you are never alone. Call unto Lord, He is always near and ready to help you and give you wisdom in every situation you may face.

If you are reading this book and you have not given your heart to the Lord Jesus, this book is for you as well. It is my intent to show you the love of Jesus Christ in these writings and that He would uphold you by the words of His power in any difficult situation that you may encounter. He loves all people, those who have accepted Him as Lord and Savior and those who have not. He will never force His will upon anyone to accept Him. He loves all people unconditionally.

Numbers 6:24-26 (NKJV)

"The LORD bless you and keep you; The LORD make His face shine upon you, And be gracious to you; The LORD lift up His countenance upon you, And give you peace."

Amen

Should you choose to surrender your life to the Lord Jesus if you feel led to do so by the Holy Spirit pleaser say this prayer.

Salvation Prayer

Father, I come before you today with a yielding heart acknowledging that I am a sinner that needs you in my life Jesus and I ask you to forgive me of all my sins and cleanse me of all unrighteousness. I have done many things that are not pleasing to you and I repent of my sins. I believe that you died on the cross for my sins and I ask you to come into my heart. Help me to live a life that will be well-pleasing to you. I receive you as my Lord and Savior in Jesus' name. If you read this prayer you have become a citizen of the kingdom of God. God bless you.

www.ingramcontent.com/pod-product-compliance
Lightning Source LLC
Chambersburg PA
CBHW071009120626
46546CB00003B/998